PEDIATRIC FIRST AID, CPR, AND AED

National Safety Council

Boston   Burr Ridge, IL   Dubuque, IA   Madison, WI   New York
San Francisco   St. Louis   Bangkok   Bogotá   Caracas   Kuala Lumpur
Lisbon   London   Madrid   Mexico City   Milan   Montreal   New Delhi
Santiago   Seoul   Singapore   Sydney   Taipei   Toronto

The McGraw·Hill Companies

Mc Graw Hill Higher Education

PEDIATRIC FIRST AID, CPR, AND AED

Published by McGraw-Hill, a business unit of The McGraw-Hill Companies, Inc., 1221 Avenue of the Americas, New York, NY 10020. Copyright © 2005 by National Safety Council. All rights reserved. No part of this publication may be reproduced or distributed in any form or by any means, or stored in a database or retrieval system, without the prior written consent of The McGraw-Hill Companies, Inc., including, but not limited to, in any network or other electronic storage or transmission, or broadcast for distance learning.

Some ancillaries, including electronic and print components, may not be available to customers outside the United States.

This book is printed on acid-free paper.

3 4 5 6 7 8 9 0 KGP/KGP 0 9 8 7 6 5

ISBN 0–07–301677–2

Publisher: *David T. Culverwell*
Senior Sponsoring Editor: *Roxan Kinsey*
Developmental Editor: *Patricia Forrest*
Editorial Coordinator: *Connie Kuhl*
Outside Managing Editor: *Kelly Trakalo*
Outside Production Editor: *Marilyn Rothenberger*
Marketing Manager: *Lynn M. Kalb*
Senior Project Manager: *Sheila M. Frank*
Senior Production Supervisor: *Laura Fuller*
Lead Media Project Manager: *Audrey A. Reiter*
Media Technology Producer: *Janna Martin*
Senior Coordinator of Freelance Design: *Michelle D. Whitaker*
Cover/Interior Designer: *Seann Dwyer/Studio Montage, St. Louis, MO*
Lead Photo Research Coordinator: *Carrie K. Burger*
Photo Research: *Karen Pugliano*
Supplement Producer: *Brenda A. Ernzen*
Compositor and Art Studio: *Electronic Publishing Services Inc., NYC*
Typeface: *11.5/13 Minion*
Printer: *Quebecor World Kingsport*

Photo Credits: Figures 3-3, 3-4, 3-6, 3-7, 5-5: Image courtesy Bradley R. Davis; Figures 3-5, 5-7, 7-2: © Mediscan; Figures 5-3, 5-4, 5-6: © Dr. P. Marazzi/Photo Researchers, Inc.; Figure 9-2a: Courtesy www.poison-ivy.org; Figure 9-2b: Image courtesy M. D. Vaden, Certified Arborist, Oregon; Figure 9-2c: © Gilbert Grant/Photo Researchers, Inc.; Figure 9-3a: Centers for Disease Control; Figure 9-3b: CDC/Harold G. Scott; Figure 9-4a: © Brad Mogen/Visuals Unlimited; Figure 9-4b: Photo by Scott Bauer, Agricultural Research Service, USDA; Figure 9-6: © Science VU/Visuals Unlimited; Figure 9-7: © DV13/Digital Vision/Getty Images; Figure 10-1a: © Mediscan; Figure 10-1b: © SIU/Visuals Unlimited; Figure 13-1: CDC/J.D. Millar; Figure 13-2: © Dr. P. Marazzi/Photo Researchers, Inc.; Figure 13-4: © Mediscan; Figure 13-5: © St. Bartholomew's Hospital/Photo Researchers, Inc.; Figure 13-6, 13-7: Centers for Disease Control; Figure 13-8: CDC/Dr. Lucille K. Georg; Figure 13-9: © Mediscan; Figure 13-10: © Dr. P. Marazzi/Photo Researchers, Inc.; Figure 13-11: © St. Bartholomew's Hospital/Photo Researchers, Inc.; all other photographs © The McGraw-Hill Companies, Inc./Rick Brady, photographer.

Illustrations by Electronic Publishing Services Inc.: Jennifer Brumbaugh – Figures 1-1, 2-4, 2-5, 2-9, 3-1, 3-2, 3-12, 4-1, 6-1; Matthew McAdams – Figures 2-1, 2-6, 3-9, 5-2, 7-1, 8-1; Jay McElroy – Figure 9-1; Evelyn Pence – Figures 2-3b, c, Figures on page 33.

The information presented in this book is based on the current recommendations of responsible medical and industrial sources at the time of printing. The National Safety Council and the publisher, however, make no guarantee as to, and assume no responsibility for, correctness, sufficiency or completeness of such information or recommendations. Other or additional safety measures may be required under particular circumstances.

www.mhhe.com

About the National Safety Council

Founded in 1913, the National Safety Council is a nonprofit membership organization devoted to protecting life and promoting health. Its mission "is to educate and influence society to adopt safety, health, and environmental policies, practices, and procedures that prevent and mitigate human suffering and economic losses arising from preventable causes."

The National Safety Council has been the leader in protecting life and promoting health in the workplace for over 90 years. The Council has helped make great improvements in workplace safety, and expanded our focus to include safety on the roads, and in the home and community. Working through its 37,000 members, and in partnership with public agencies, private groups, and other associations, the Council serves as an impartial information gathering and distribution organization; it disseminates safety, health, and environmental materials from its Itasca, Illinois, headquarters through a network of regional offices, chapters, and training centers.

In 1990 we established First Aid and CPR courses to promote effective emergency response. Since then, we have grown to meet the changing needs of emergency responders at all levels of expertise. Upon successful completion of this course, you join more than 10 million National Safety Council trained responders protecting life and promoting health.

Acknowledgements

The National Safety Council wishes to thank the following Chapters and individuals for their assistance in developing this program:

For providing technical advice and assistance with photography: Safety Council of Maryland and Ms. Pat Raven, Director, Occupational Services, Safety Council of Maryland.

For providing technical advice and assistance with videotaping: the Arizona Chapter, National Safety Council, John Stubbs and C. J. Anderson.

For providing technical writing services: Tom Lochhaas, Editorial Services, Newburyport, MA.

For providing direction and support for National Safety Council Emergency Care programs: Donna M. Siegfried, Executive Director, Emergency Care & Home and Community Programs; Barbara Caracci, Director of Emergency Care Products and Training; Donna Fredenhagen, Manager of National Programs and Initiatives; Kathy Safranek, Project Administrator.

Publisher's Acknowledgements

Jason Goetz
Senior Safety Engineer
Worldwide Environmental, Health & Safety
Intel Corporation
Phoenix, AZ

James H. Howson
Director, Emergency Preparedness
New Jersey Hospital
Princeton, NJ

Tom Link
Safety and Health Council of North Carolina
Harrisburg, NC

Robb Rehberg, Ph.D.
Director and Chief, Emergency Medical Services
Montclair State University
Upper Montclair, NJ

B. Drew Wellmon, D.O.
Wellmon Family Practice
Shippensburg, PA

Table of Contents

Introduction

Why Learn Injury Prevention and First Aid?

Injuries are the number one health problem for children in the United States. Injuries to infants and children vary from simple cuts and bruises to life-threatening emergencies. According to the National SAFE KIDS Campaign, following are the most common injuries leading to death in children at different ages:

Infants (0–1 years)

1. Choking
2. Motor vehicle occupant injury
3. Drowning
4. Fires and burns

Children (1–4 years)

1. Drowning
2. Motor vehicle occupant injury
3. Pedestrian injuries
4. Fires and burns
5. Choking

Children (5–14 years)

1. Motor vehicle occupant injury
2. Pedestrian injuries
3. Drowning
4. Fires and burns
5. Bicycle injuries

Each year more than six million children under age 14 are treated in emergency rooms for unintentional injuries. Tragically, about 5,000 children die every year from their injuries. Tens of thousands more have permanent disabilities resulting from their injuries.

COMMON CHILDHOOD INJURIES
- Falls
- Struck by/against
- Overexertion
- Bite/sting
- Cut/pierce
- Poisoning
- Motor vehicle occupant
- Bicycle injury
- Airway obstruction from foreign object
- Fire/burn

(Adapted from National Safety Council, *Injury Facts, 2003 edition*)

PREVENTING INJURIES IN CHILDHOOD

It has been estimated that 90% of all injuries to infants and children could have been prevented. Obviously, prevention is a better solution than simply being prepared to give first aid once an injury has occurred. Chapters 15 and 16 describe guidelines you can follow to prevent injuries and ensure your childcare center, home, school, and other settings are safe for infants and children.

WHAT IS FIRST AID?

First aid is the immediate help given to a child who is injured or experiences sudden illness by an adult, usually a caretaker, until appropriate medical help arrives or the child is seen by a healthcare provider. First aid often is not the only treatment the child needs, but it helps the child for the usually short time until advanced care begins.

Most first aid is fairly simple and does not require extensive training or equipment. With the first aid training in this course and a basic first aid kit, you can perform first aid.

Goals of First Aid

- Keep the child alive
- Prevent the child's condition from getting worse
- Help promote the child's recovery from the injury or illness
- Ensure the child receives medical care
- Keep the child calm and distracted while providing care

THE EMERGENCY MEDICAL SERVICES SYSTEM

People who are trained in first aid are the first step in the Emergency Medical Services (EMS) system. As a first aider you are *only* the first step, so part of your responsibility is to make sure the EMS system responds to help a child with a serious injury or sudden illness by calling 911 (or your local or company emergency number). You will learn more about calling EMS in Chapter 1.

In most communities in the United States, help will arrive within minutes. The first aid you give helps the child until then.

BE PREPARED

- ***Know what to do.*** This first aid course will teach you what to do.
- ***Stay ready.*** A first aid situation can occur to a child at any time and in any place. Think of yourself as a first aider who is always ready to step in and help. You should always feel confident that you can help an injured or ill child.
- ***Have a personal first aid kit, and know where kits are kept in your childcare center, home, or other setting.*** Be sure first aid kits are well stocked with the right supplies. Keep emergency phone numbers, such as EMS, the Poison Control Center, and other emergency agencies, in a handy place.
- ***Know whether your community uses 911 or a different emergency telephone number.*** Note that this manual says "Call 911" throughout. If your community does not use the 911 system, call your local emergency number instead.

PREVENTING EMERGENCIES

Remember that many injuries can be prevented, and always take the appropriate steps to ensure places where children are present are safe for them. Learn to be watchful for any hazards in the environment—do not wait for a problem to arise before acting to eliminate hazards and risks to children.

DISASTER PREPAREDNESS

Whether you are a parent or childcare provider, you should also be prepared in case of natural disaster and other incidents. In some states, such preparedness is required for childcare providers.

Childcare providers must be prepared for catastrophic emergencies such as earthquake, flood, and fire. Be prepared to evacuate areas, and know how to respond if basic services such as water, gas, electricity, or telephones are disrupted.

Childcare providers should have an action plan for these types of emergencies. This plan can be prepared with the assistance of local EMS, fire, and/or law enforcement authorities.

The Federal Emergency Management Agency (FEMA) provides these basic guidelines if a disaster occurs:

- Use flashlights, not matches, candles, or other open flames. Do not turn on electrical switches if you suspect damage.
- Sniff for gas leaks and if suspected, turn off the main gas valve, open windows, and evacuate.
- Turn off any other damaged utilities.
- Clean up any flammable liquids immediately.
- Have a plan that details your evacuation process and routes.
- Maintain a disaster kit that includes a supply of water, infant- or child-appropriate food, first aid kit, clothing, bedding, tools, emergency supplies, and special items such as individual medications. Keep the items that you would most likely need during an evacuation in an easy-to-carry container such as a backpack.
- Store water in plastic containers. Generally, children will need more than two quarts of drinking water per day.
- Store at least a three-day supply of non-perishable food such as high-energy bars, or ready-to-eat canned meats, fruits, and vegetables.

If you are employed in a childcare center, you should know other guidelines required at your center.

YOUR FIRST AID KIT

A well-stocked first aid kit should be present in your home, vehicle, and childcare center. Take one with you on activities such as camping and boating. A cell phone is also helpful in most emergencies.

Ensure the first aid kit is in a locked container kept where children cannot access it. In a childcare center, all adults should know where the kit is kept. The contents of the kit should be checked regularly, and all items should be replaced as used. Medicines taken by individual children should not be kept in the first aid kit but locked safely in another location.

Make sure your first aid kit includes the items shown in Figure I-1. Note that you may not necessarily use all items in a kit just because they are there. For example, first aiders other than a child's parents or authorized childcare provider generally do not give medications such

Learning Checkpoint ①

1. True or False: When you give a child first aid, that child does not then need to see a healthcare provider.

2. True or False: First aid given promptly can save lives and reduce the severity of injuries.

3. Being prepared for an emergency means:

   a. Knowing what to do

   b. Being ready to act anytime, anywhere

   c. Knowing how to get medical care for an injured or ill child

   d. All of the above

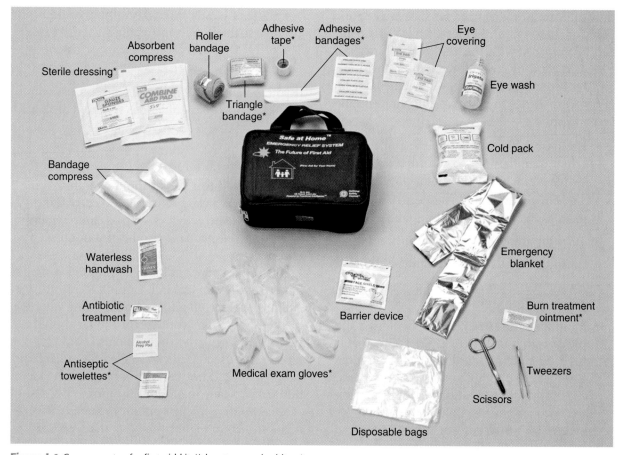

Figure I-1 Components of a first aid kit (*denotes required item).

as prescription or over-the-counter pain medication (for example, acetaminophen).

In addition to these first aid kit items, other items may be required. In California, for example, first aid kits in childcare centers must include a flashlight with extra batteries, pen and paper, and activated charcoal.

LEGAL ISSUES

Can You Be Sued for Giving First Aid?

Generally you do not need to be concerned about being sued for giving first aid. If you give first aid as you are trained in this course, and do your best, there is little chance of being found legally liable. To protect yourself always follow these guidelines:

1. Act *only* as you are trained to act.
2. Have permission to give first aid.
3. Do not move an injured child unnecessarily.
4. Call for professional help.
5. Keep giving care until help arrives.

Must You Give First Aid?

In general, in most states you have no legal obligation to give first aid as a citizen or a bystander at the scene of an emergency. As the specific obligations may vary, ask your instructor about the law in your area. If you do begin giving first aid, however, it is important to note that you are obligated to continue giving care if you can and to remain with the victim.

In certain situations, however, you may have a legal obligation to give first aid. If you work as a childcare provider and giving first aid is part of your job, you have a legal responsibility to act appropriately. This is called a **duty to act.** If you are employed as a childcare provider and are unsure of your role in emergencies, talk with your employer to be sure you know your specific responsibilities.

In addition to employed childcare providers, parents and guardians also have a legal responsibility to give first aid to children in their care. This is called a pre-existing relationship and involves a legal responsibility. A pre-existing relationship also includes adults overseeing children in any situation, such as an adult who is transporting children in a vehicle or watching them at a playground.

As noted before, once you begin giving first aid, in any situation, you are obligated to continue giving care until emergency medical help takes over, another trained rescuer takes over, or you become physically exhausted.

Good Samaritan Laws

Most states have laws called **Good Samaritan laws** designed to encourage people to help others in an emergency without worrying about being sued. These laws protect adults who give first aid to other adults or children in their care, except for those employed in childcare. It is unlikely you would be found liable or financially responsible for a child's injury as long as you follow the guidelines described in this book. Ask your instructor about the specific Good Samaritan laws in your area.

Get Consent

You must have permission in order to give first aid. If you are employed at a childcare center, the center should already have the parents' permission to give emergency and other first aid to their children.

If you are the responsible adult supervising children in any other setting, and the child's parents or guardians are not present when a child is injured or becomes ill, you are assumed to have the parent's or guardian's permission to give emergency care. In a nonemergency situation you should try to reach a parent or guardian to get his or her permission, but in an emergency consent is assumed. This is called **implied consent.**

You may also encounter emergencies with adult victims of injury or sudden illness. A responsive (awake and alert) victim must give permission before you can give first aid. Tell the person you have been trained and describe what you will do to help. The victim may give permission by telling you it is okay or by nodding agreement. An unresponsive victim, however, is assumed to give consent for your help. Again, this is called implied consent.

Follow Standards of Care

Legally, you may be liable for the results of your actions if you do not follow accepted standards of care. **Standard of care** refers to what others with your same training would do in a similar situation. It is important that when you give first aid, do only as you are trained. Any other actions could result in the injury or illness becoming worse.

You may be guilty of **negligence** if:

1. You have a duty to act (as a childcare provider, parent or guardian, or adult with a pre-existing relationship with a child).
2. You breach that duty (by not acting or acting incorrectly).
3. Your actions or inaction causes injury or damages (including such things as physical injury or pain).

Examples of negligent actions could include moving a victim unnecessarily, doing something you have not been trained to do, or failing to give first aid as you have been trained.

Remember, once you begin giving first aid, do not stop until another trained person takes over. Stay with the victim until help arrives. If you leave the victim and the injury or illness becomes worse, this is called **abandonment.** Note that abandonment is different from justified instances of stopping care, such as if you are exhausted and unable to continue or you are in imminent danger because of hazards at the scene.

Documentation

A final legal responsibility in some childcare situations is documenting the child's injury or illness and the care you gave. Some states require such documentation. In California, for example, a special form must be filled out anytime a child receives professional medical care (including EMS personnel) while in a licensed childcare home or facility. Check with your employer about any state or facility policies for documentation.

Even if not legally required, it is a good idea whenever caring for children not your own to write down what happened and what you did. This information may be important for the child's parents or guardians and for healthcare providers who later treat the child.

COPING WITH A TRAUMATIC EVENT

Emergencies are stressful, especially with injured or ill children. When a child is seriously injured or does not survive, the incident can be traumatic for caregivers. It is important to realize that not even medical professionals can save every victim. Some injuries, illness, or circumstances are often beyond our control. If you experience such an emergency, you may have a strong reaction, or later on you may have problems coping. This is normal—we are only human, after all. To help cope with the effects of a traumatic event:

- Talk to others: family members, coworkers, local emergency responders, or your family healthcare provider (without breaching confidentiality of the victim)
- Remind yourself your reaction is normal
- Do not be afraid or reluctant to ask for professional help. If you have an Employee Assistance Program or Member Assistance Program, they often can provide such help. Ask your personal healthcare provider who you can talk to for help.

Learning
Checkpoint ②

1. True or False: Good Samaritan laws protect only professionals like paramedics and health-care providers.

2. True or False: The best thing to do in any emergency is move the child to your car and get him or her to an emergency room.

3. You have a duty to act when:

   a. You stop at the scene of an emergency

   b. You have taken a first aid course

   c. You have a first aid kit with you

   d. Your job requires you to give first aid when needed

4. Check off which victims you have permission to give first aid to:

   ___a. An unresponsive adult victim

   ___b. A child without a parent or guardian present

   ___c. All victims, all of the time

   ___d. An adult victim who nods when you ask if it is okay to give first aid

   ___e. A child whose parent or guardian gives consent for the child

5. Check off things you should always do when giving first aid:

___**a.** Move the child

___**b.** Do what you have been trained to do

___**c.** Try any first aid technique you have read or heard about

___**d.** Be sure you have permission

___**e.** Stay with the child until another trained person takes over

___**f.** Transport all children to the emergency room in your vehicle

1 Take Action in an Emergency

This chapter describes actions to take in all emergencies involving injury or illness. Always follow these basic steps:

1. Recognize the emergency and check the scene.
2. Prepare to help.
3. Call 911 (when appropriate).
4. Check the injured or ill child.
5. Give first aid.
6. Ensure the injured or ill child sees a healthcare provider (when appropriate).

Later chapters describe the specific first aid to give in different situations. This chapter describes the six steps above, how to protect yourself from infectious disease when giving first aid, and how to assess an injured or ill child.

WHAT YOU CAN DO

In any emergency, try to stay calm and confident. Remember your training. Acting calmly and confidently will help calm the injured or ill child as well.

In a childcare situation, in which other children and adults are likely to be present, consider the complete situation and others involved. While it is important to care for the injured or ill child in your care, it is also important to properly handle others who may be affected by the incident. Calm and reassure parents during an emergency with their child. Tell the parent(s) that you are trained to handle the emergency situation and what you are doing to help their child. Calm and

reassure other children as well. Whenever possible, have another childcare provider supervise the other children while you provide care for the ill or injured child. Explain that you will talk with the children about what happened as soon as possible and answer their questions.

Follow these six steps in any emergency:

Recognize the Emergency and Check the Scene

You usually know there is an emergency when you see one. You see an injured or ill child, or a child acting strangely. Or you may not see a victim at first but see signs that an emergency has occurred and that someone may be hurt.

Although most childcare situations do not involve hazards to yourself and others, such hazards may be present. Always check the scene when you recognize an emergency has occurred—before rushing in to help the victim. This is particularly important when outdoors or in unfamiliar settings. You must be safe yourself if you are to help another. Look for any hazards such as the following:

- Smoke, flames
- Spilled chemicals, fumes
- Downed electrical wires
- Risk of explosion, building collapse
- Roadside dangers, high-speed traffic
- Potential personal violence

If the scene is dangerous, *stay away and call for help.* Do not become a victim yourself!

As part of checking the scene, look to see if other children are injured or ill. More help may be needed for multiple victims. Check that all children are present and make sure you are not overlooking other injuries. Look also for any clues that may help you determine what happened and what first aid may be needed. As well, look for other adults who may be able to help give first aid or go to a telephone to call 911.

Decide to Help

When you see an injured child and have determined the scene is safe, you need to act. This is not always easy. Although you may be worried about not doing the right thing, remember that you have first aid training. Once you call for help, medical professionals will be there very soon. Your goal is to help the victim until they take over.

Call 911

Call 911 (or your local emergency number) immediately if you recognize a life-threatening injury or illness. A life-threatening emergency is one in which a problem threatens the child's airway, breathing, or circulation of blood, as described later in this chapter. Do not try to transport a child to the emergency room yourself in such cases. Movement may worsen the child's condition, or the child may suddenly need ad-

ditional care on the way. If you are not sure whether a situation is serious enough to call, don't hesitate—call 911. It is better to be safe than sorry (**Figure 1-1**).

If the child is responsive and may not be seriously injured or ill, go on to the next step to check the child before calling 911—and then call 911 if needed.

Always call 911 when:

- The child may have a life-threatening condition
- The child is unresponsive
- The child's condition may become life threatening
- Moving the child could make the condition worse

Later chapters on first aid describe when to call 911 for other specific problems.

In addition to calling 911 for injury or illness, call in these situations:

- Fire, explosion
- Vehicle crash
- Downed electrical wire
- Chemical spill, gas leak, or the presence of any unknown substances

How to Call EMS

When you call 911 or your local emergency number, be ready to give the following information:

- Your name and the phone number you are using
- The location and number of injured or ill children—specific enough for the arriving crew to find them
- What happened to the child and any special circumstances or conditions that may require special rescue or medical equipment
- The child's condition: For example, is the child responsive? Breathing? Bleeding?
- The child's approximate age and sex
- What is being done for the child

It is important to not hang up until the dispatcher instructs you to, because you may be given advice on how to care for the child.

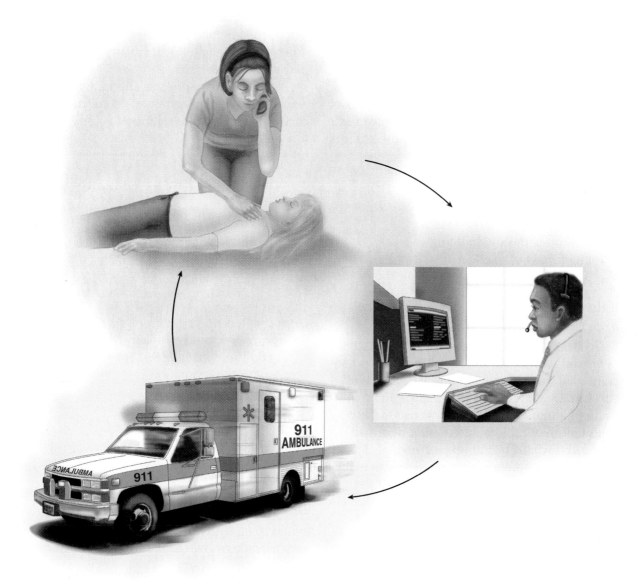

Figure 1-1 Call 911.

If other adults are present, ask them to call 911 while you go on to check the child and give first aid.

Check the Victim

First check the child and correct for life-threatening conditions requiring immediate first aid (see later section "Check the ABCs").

Give First Aid

Give first aid once you have checked the child and know his or her condition. Later chapters give the first aid steps for the conditions you are likely to find. In many cases first aid involves simple actions you can take to help the victim.

Get the Victim to a Healthcare Provider

You may have decided at first that the child's condition was not an emergency and did not call 911. In many cases, however, the child still needs to see a healthcare provider. If you have any doubt, call 911. If you are employed in a childcare center, follow your center's policy regarding contacting the child's parents. Later

Learning
Checkpoint ①

1. True or False: If you see a child injured in an emergency, the first thing to do is get to the child quickly and check his or her condition.

2. When you encounter an injured victim, you should:

   a. Give first aid until help arrives

   b. Help a victim only if the scene is safe

   c. Call 911 for life-threatening injuries

   d. All of the above

3. Call 911 for:

   a. Medical problems only

   b. Police and fire services only

   c. Medical problems and fires only

   d. Medical problems and all emergencies

chapters on specific conditions requiring first aid describe when a victim needs to go to the emergency room or see a healthcare provider.

AVOIDING INFECTION

In any emergency situation there is some risk of a first aider getting an infectious disease from a victim who has a disease. That risk is very low, however, and taking steps to prevent being infected greatly reduces that risk. You can take precautions to prevent transmission of blood-borne and airborne infectious diseases.

Bloodborne Disease

Several serious diseases can be transmitted from one person to another through contact with the infected person's blood. These are called blood-borne diseases. Bacteria or viruses that cause such diseases, called pathogens, are also present in some other body fluids, such as semen, vaginal secretions, and bloody saliva or vomit. Other body fluids, such as nasal secretions, sweat, tears, and urine, do not normally transmit pathogens.

Three serious bloodborne infections are HIV, hepatitis B, and hepatitis C.

HIV

The human immunodeficiency virus (HIV) is the pathogen that eventually causes AIDS (acquired immunodeficiency syndrome). AIDS is a fatal disease transmitted from one person to another only through body fluids.

Because HIV can be transmitted through pregnancy and occasionally through breast milk, some children in childcare situations may have the virus. There have been no known cases, however, of the virus spreading from one child to another in childcare settings or schools. Nonetheless, childcare providers should always take precautions when blood or body fluids of *any* child or adult victim are involved (see following section).

Note that a child's medical record is confidential. If you are employed in a childcare center, follow your center's policies when caring for a child known to have the HIV virus.

Remember that HIV is transmitted only through body fluids. It is not spread through regular daily activities such as touching, coughing or sneezing, sharing foods, sharing a restroom, or playing together.

Hepatitis B

Hepatitis B (HBV) is a viral infectious disease of the liver transmitted through contact with an infected person's body fluids. The disease is difficult to treat and often remains in the person for life, possibly leading to liver damage or cancer.

A vaccine is available for HBV. Individuals who are more likely to come in contact with HBV-infected people, such as healthcare workers and professional rescuers, often get this vaccine. The law requires that such employees who are at risk for HBV be offered free vaccinations by their employer.

Hepatitis C

Hepatitis C (HCV) is another bloodborne viral disease that can cause liver disease or cancer. It cannot be cured, and there is no vaccine. Following the same precautions to protect against transmission of HIV will also prevent transmission of HBV and HCV.

WEST NILE VIRUS

West Nile Virus (WNV) is a relatively new bloodborne disease now established as a seasonal epidemic in parts of North America. Less than 1% of people infected with WNV develop severe illness, however, and about 80% have no signs and symptoms at all. WNV is spread mostly by the bite of infected mosquitoes. The best way to avoid WNV is to prevent mosquito bites with personal protection, such as wearing long sleeves and pants and reducing mosquito breeding sites.

Protection Against Bloodborne Disease

Because these bloodborne diseases cannot be cured, they should be prevented. The best prevention is to avoid contact with *all* vic-

tims' blood and body fluids. You cannot know whether a child or other victim (even a close friend) may be infected, because often these diseases do not produce signs and symptoms. Even the victim may not know that he or she is infected.

The Centers for Disease Control and Prevention (CDC) therefore recommends taking **universal precautions** whenever giving first aid. *Universal* means for all victims, all the time. Always assume that blood and body fluids may be infected. Use the following recommended precautions to prevent coming into contact with a victim's blood or body fluids:

- Use personal protective equipment
- If you do not have medical exam gloves with you, put your hands in plastic bags or use another barrier between you and the blood or body fluid
- Wash your hands with soap and water before and after giving first aid
- Cover any cuts or scrapes in your skin with protective clothing or gloves
- Do not touch your mouth, nose, or eyes when giving first aid (e.g., do not eat, drink, or smoke)
- Do not touch objects soiled with blood or body fluids
- Be careful to avoid being cut by anything sharp at the emergency scene, such as broken glass or torn metal
- Use absorbent material to soak up spilled blood or body fluids, and dispose of appropriately; clean the area with a commercial disinfectant or a freshly made 10% bleach solution
- If you are exposed to a victim's blood or body fluid, wash immediately with soap and water and call your healthcare provider. At work, report the situation to your supervisor

See also Chapter 14 on preventing illness in childcare settings (available from your instructor).

Personal Protective Equipment

Personal protective equipment (PPE) is any equipment used to protect yourself from contact with blood or other body fluids. Most important, keep medical exam gloves in your first aid kit and wear them in most first aid situations (**Figure 1-2**).

Latex Gloves

Medical exam gloves are often made of latex rubber, to which some people are allergic. Signs and symptoms of latex allergy may include skin rashes, hives, itching skin or eyes, flushing, watering or swollen eyes, a runny nose, or an asthmatic reaction. Use gloves made of vinyl or other material if you have any of these symptoms or if you know the victim has a latex allergy.

A pocket face mask or face shield is a barrier device used when giving rescue breathing or CPR. This device should be in the first aid kit, and you should always use it for added protection. Because giving rescue breathing with a barrier device can greatly reduce the chance of an infectious disease being transmitted from or to a victim, barrier devices are always recommended (**Figure 1-3**).

Airborne Disease

Infectious diseases may also be transmitted through the air, especially from a victim who is coughing or sneezing. Tuberculosis (TB)

has made a comeback in the last decade and is sometimes resistant to treatment.

Healthcare workers use precautions when caring for people known or suspected to have TB, but rarely does a first aider need to take special precautions against airborne disease.

In 2003 an outbreak of severe acute respiratory syndrome (SARS) in some parts of the world caused a new scare. SARS is primarily an airborne infectious disease, transmitted when an infected person coughs or sneezes within close proximity to others. During the 2003 epidemic almost 10% of the approximately 8000 known SARS victims in the world died. Only 7 people in the U.S. were known to have contracted SARS, however, all caused by international travel to epidemic areas. The CDC continues to monitor the risks of SARS and will issue updates and warnings if new outbreaks occur.

First aiders who want to learn more about preventing bloodborne and airborne disease are encouraged to take the National Safety Council course on Bloodborne and Airborne Pathogens.

CHECK THE INJURED OR ILL CHILD

As described earlier, after you recognize the emergency, check the scene for safety, and call 911 if appropriate, you then check the child to see what problems may need first aid. This check, called an **assessment,** has three steps:

1. Check for immediate life-threatening conditions (check the ABCs).

Figure 1-2. Wear gloves to protect yourself from contact with blood or other body fluids.

Figure 1-3. Variety of barrier devices.

Learning
Checkpoint ②

1. True or False: Bloodborne diseases are transmitted only through contact with an infected person's blood.

2. True or False: The risk of getting a serious infectious disease by giving first aid is greatly reduced when you take precautions.

3. "Universal precautions" means:

   a. Treat all victims as if their body fluids were infected

   b. Always wear gloves if blood may be present

   c. Do not touch your mouth, nose, or eyes when giving first aid

   d. All of the above

4. Check off which of the following situations could lead to getting an infectious disease:

   _____ **a.** Touching a bloody bandage in a trash can

   _____ **b.** Touching a child with HIV

   _____ **c.** Receiving a hepatitis B vaccination

   _____ **d.** Not wearing gloves and giving first aid if you have a cut on your finger

   _____ **e.** Being near a person with hepatitis C who is coughing

   _____ **f.** Contact with an unresponsive victim

---

2. Get the victim's history (find out what happened and what may have contributed to the emergency).

3. Check the rest of the child's body (perform a physical examination).

While giving first aid and waiting for help to arrive, continue with a fourth step:

4. Monitor the child for any changes.

Always perform these steps in this order. If there is an immediate life-threatening problem, such as stopped breathing, the child needs immediate help. This victim could die if you first spent time looking for broken bones or asking bystanders what happened. *Always remember:* Check the ABCs first!

Check the ABCs

In less than a minute you can check the child for immediate life-threatening conditions. This is called "checking the ABCs," where:

   A = Airway

   B = Breathing

   C = Circulation

We need these three things functioning to stay alive.

Begin your check of the ABCs by speaking to the child as you approach. **If the child can speak or cough or is crying, then the airway is open, the child is breathing, and the heart is beating.**

Unless the child is obviously alert, **check for responsiveness.** Tap the child on the shoulder and ask if he or she is okay or flick the heels of an infant. A child is responsive if he or she speaks to you, moves purposefully, or otherwise responds to stimuli. A child who does not respond is called unresponsive. An unresponsive child is considered to have a potentially life-threatening condition. Immediately call for help so that someone calls 911. If the victim is unresponsive, continue checking the ABCs.

A = Airway

We can breathe only if our airway is open. The airway may be blocked by something stuck in the throat or by an unresponsive child's own tongue. The most common cause of an obstructed airway in an unresponsive child is the tongue. To make sure the tongue is not obstructing the airway, position the unresponsive child's head to open the airway. Carefully position the child on his or her back, keeping the head and neck in line with the body as you roll the child as one unit. In a child not suspected of having a neck injury, tilt the head back and lift the chin. This is called the head tilt-chin lift (**Figure 1-4**).

If the child may have a neck or spine injury (see Chapter 6), do not tilt the head back to open the airway. Instead, only lift the jaw upward using both hands. This is called a jaw thrust (**Figure 1-5**).

B = Breathing

After opening the airway, you then check to see if the child is breathing. **Look** at the child's chest to see if it rises and falls with breathing. Lean over with your ear close to the child's mouth and nose and **listen** for any sounds of breathing. You may also **feel** breath on your cheek. If you do not notice any signs of breathing within 10 seconds, assume the child is not breathing.

At this point, using a barrier device if available (see Chapter 2), give two slow breaths to a child who is not breathing. Watch for a rise and fall in the child's chest to ensure your breath is entering the lungs. If the breaths do not go in, attempt to reposition the airway to ensure it is open and try again. If the breaths still do not go in, give care for choking (see Chapter 2).

C = Circulation

If the child's airway is open and the child is breathing, or you are breathing for the child, you next check for circulation. This means checking that the heart is beating and blood is moving around the body (circulating). If the child's heart has stopped or the child is bleeding profusely, there is a circulation problem and the child can die. **If the child is moving, coughing, speaking, crying, or breathing, the heart is beating.**

Check for signs of circulation by scanning the body for any signs of breathing, coughing, movement, and normal skin condition. Lack of circulation may be indicated by bluish, pale skin color, cool skin temperature, and clammy skin. It is currently recommended that *only healthcare workers or professional rescuers spend time checking for a victim's pulse.* Check for severe bleeding by quickly looking over the child's body for obvious blood. Control any severe bleeding with direct pressure (see Chapter 3).

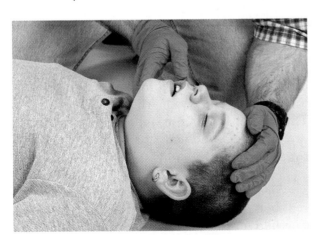

Figure 1-4 Head tilt-chin lift.

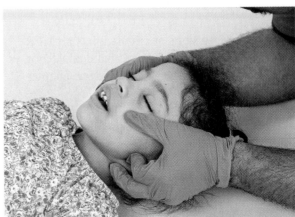

Figure 1-5 Jaw thrust.

Perform the Skill

Check the ABCs

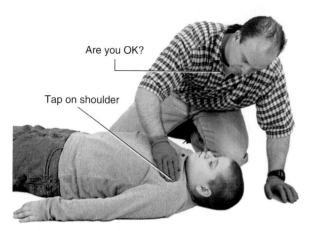

Are you OK?

Tap on shoulder

1 Check responsiveness.

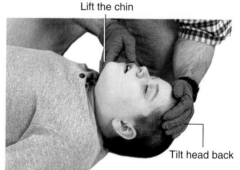

Lift the chin

Tilt head back

2 Open the airway.

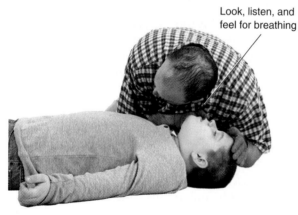

Look, listen, and feel for breathing

3 Check for breathing.

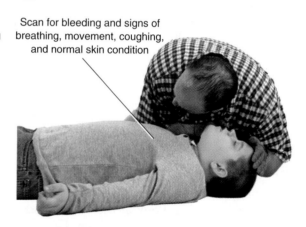

Scan for bleeding and signs of breathing, movement, coughing, and normal skin condition

4 Check for signs of circulation.

If you see no signs of circulation, start CPR and call for an automated external defibrillator (AED) to be brought to the scene (see Chapter 2).

Get a History

After checking the child's ABCs, if you find no immediate life-threatening conditions you must care for, continue to check the child for other problems and try to find out more about what happened. Ask the child simple questions such as "What happened?" and "Where does it hurt?"

Ask other people about what they know or saw.

It is important to try to get information about the child and the problem, called "the history," to help you decide what first aid to give. This information is also important for health-care providers who may later treat the child. Use the **SAMPLE** history format:

S = Signs and symptoms. What can you observe about the child's problem (**signs**)? Ask the child how he or she feels (**symptoms**).

A = *Allergies.* Ask an older child or a parent about any allergies to foods, medicines, insect stings, or other substances. Look for a medical ID bracelet. In a childcare setting, someone can check the child's file for such information (**Figure 1-6**).

M = *Medications.* Find out if the child is taking any prescribed medications or over-the-counter products.

P = *Previous problems.* Find out if the child has had a problem like this before or has any other illnesses.

L = *Last food or drink.* Find out what and when the child last ate or drank.

E = *Events.* Ask the child and others what happened and try to identify the events that led to the current situation.

Physical Examination

The third step of the assessment of an injured or ill child is the physical examination. With this examination you may find other injuries that need first aid or additional clues to a child's condition. It is important to note, however, that you do not stop giving first aid for a serious condition just to do this examination. Instead, keep the child still and calm and wait for EMS professionals.

The physical examination includes examining the child from toe to head looking for any-

Figure 1-6. Examples of medical ID jewelry.

thing out of the ordinary. Starting at the toes and working up to the head allows a child to get used to you in a more nonthreatening manner. As a general rule look for the following signs and symptoms of injury or illness throughout the body:

- Pain when an area is touched
- Bleeding or wounds
- An area that is swollen or deformed from its usual appearance
- Skin color (flushed or pale), temperature (hot or cold), moisture (dry, sweating, clammy)
- Abnormal sensation or movement of the area

Monitor the Child

Give first aid for injuries or illness you discover as you assess the child. With very minor conditions the child may need no more than your first aid. In other situations the child may need to see a healthcare provider or go to an emergency room. With all life-threatening or serious conditions, you should have called 911 and are now awaiting the arrival of help.

While waiting for help, stay with the child and make sure his or her condition does not worsen. With an unresponsive child or a victim with a serious injury, check the ABCs at least every five minutes.

MOVING A CHILD

Never move a seriously injured or ill child unless you have to for his or her own safety. Movement can worsen the condition. Wait for the arriving crew to move the child with their appropriate equipment and training.

If the scene is unsafe, you may need to move an injured or ill child. For example, you may need to remove a child from the risk of fire or poisoning by toxic fumes. If the child is not suspected to have a spinal injury and is not too heavy, you can carry the child away from the danger. Lift with your legs rather than your back, and hold the child close to your body for support.

Perform the Skill

Physical Examination of Injured Child

Feel each leg from toes to thighs for sensation, pain, deformity, and bleeding. Check feet for signs of circulation

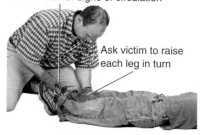

Ask victim to raise each leg in turn

1 Check lower extremities.

Ask victim to move arm. Check from shoulder to fingers for sensation, pain, deformity, and bleeding

Ask victim to shrug shoulders

2 Check upper extremities. Look for medical ID bracelet.

Gently sqeeze pelvis to detect pain or deformity

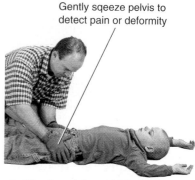

3 Check pelvis and hips.

Gently check for rigidity, pain, or bleeding

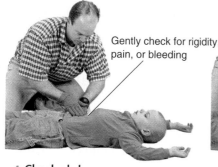

4 Check abdomen.

Check for movement of breathing, pain, deformity, and wounds

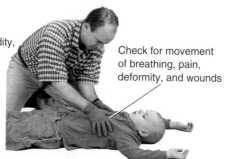

5 Check chest. Ask victim to breathe deeply.

6 Check skin appearance, temperature, moisture.

Do not move the neck

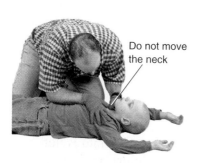

7 Check neck area for medical ID necklace, deformity or swelling, and pain.

Check pupils: equal size, react to light

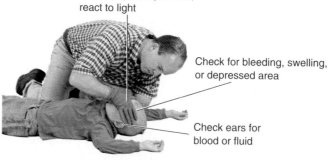

Check for bleeding, swelling, or depressed area

Check ears for blood or fluid

8 Being careful not to move the child's head or neck, check the head. If you find any problems in any body area, do not let the victim move. Wait for help to arrive.

If you think the child may have a spinal injury, you must support the head and neck in line with the body when moving the child. One way to do this, if you are alone, is with the shoulder or clothes drag, using your forearms to support the child's head while pulling him or her away from the danger (**Figure 1-7**).

(a) One-person carry

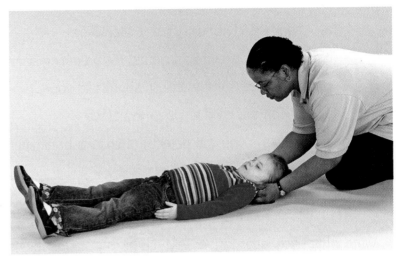

(b) Clothes drag

Figure 1-7 Emergency moves for children.

Learning
Checkpoint ③

---

1. You first encounter a child lying quietly on the floor. Number the following actions in the correct order.

_____ **a.** Check the child for signs of circulation

_____ **b.** Listen near the child's mouth for breathing sounds

_____ **c.** Check to see if the child responds to your voice or touch

_____ **d.** Position the child to open the airway

2. Describe three ways you can detect if a child is breathing.

_____

3. True or False: If you hear a child coughing or breathing, you can assume the heart is beating.

4. Write what each letter in the SAMPLE history stands for:

S = _____

A = _____

M = _____

P = _____

L = _____

E = _____

5. Describe what signs and symptoms of injury you are looking for as you examine each part of a child's body.

_____

6. As you do a physical examination of an unresponsive child, what one body area should you be very careful not to move?

_____

2 Basic Life Support

Basic life support (BLS) refers to first aid given if the victim's breathing or heart stops. Many things can cause breathing or the heart to stop. BLS is often needed for victims of:

- Heart problems
- Drowning
- Choking
- Other injuries or conditions that affect breathing or the heart

If a child's heart stops beating, breathing will stop too. If breathing stops first for any reason, the heart will stop within a few minutes. The skills you will learn in this chapter, therefore, are closely related. Rescue breathing, for example, is used by itself when a child stops breathing but still has a heart beat, and rescue breathing is used along with chest compressions (cardiopulmonary resuscitation [CPR]) if the heart stops beating.

OVERVIEW OF BLS

Giving BLS involves one or more life-saving skills, depending on the child's needs. These skills are sometimes called **resuscitation** and include:

- *Rescue breathing* to get needed oxygen into the lungs
- *Choking care,* including chest compressions, to expel an obstructing object from the airway
- *Chest compressions* to pump oxygenated blood to vital organs
- Use of an *automated external defibrillator (AED)* to shock the heart to beat regularly

Pediatric Differences

Because of size and other differences, BLS skills are used somewhat differently in children and infants than in adults. Differences in how BLS is performed occur with rescue breathing, choking, CPR, and AED, as described throughout this chapter. The exact technique to use depends on the child's age. Standard age groups are defined in the following way:

Infant — birth to 1 year
Child — ages 1 to 8
Adult — over age 8

Table 2-1 at the end of this chapter summarizes the differences in techniques among adults, children, and infants.

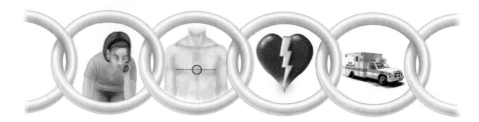

Figure 2-1 Cardiac chain of survival.

Cardiac Chain of Survival

BLS includes care given to any victim whose breathing or circulation stops. Circulation stops when the heart stops beating, a condition called **cardiac arrest.** In adults, the most common cause of sudden cardiac arrest is heart attack. Fortunately, heart attack and other heart problems are very rare in children, although other causes such as choking are more common than in adults. Causes of sudden cardiac arrest in children include such things as:

- Choking (if breathing is not restored quickly)
- Drowning
- Poisoning
- Electrocution
- Traumatic injury
- Heart problems

To recognize the urgent need for quick actions to save the life of someone whose heart has stopped, the Citizen CPR Foundation created the concept of the cardiac **chain of survival.** This chain has four crucial links (**Figure 2-1**):

1. *Early Access.* Recognize that a victim whose heart has stopped *needs help immediately!* Call 911 and get help on the way.
2. *Early CPR.* For a victim without signs of circulation (breathing, coughing, movement, normal skin condition), start CPR immediately. This helps keep the brain and other vital organs supplied with oxygen.
3. *Early Defibrillation.* An AED, now present in many places, can help get the heart beating normally again in many victims with cardiac

arrest. Send someone right away to get the AED.
4. *Early Advanced Care.* The sooner the victim is treated by emergency care professionals, the better the chance for survival. You can help make sure the victim reaches this last link in the chain by acting immediately.

THE RECOVERY POSITION

An unresponsive child who is breathing when found or after receiving BLS should be put in the recovery position. This position:

- Helps keep the airway open
- Allows fluids to drain from the mouth
- Prevents inhaling stomach contents if the child vomits

Once in the recovery position, continue to monitor the child's breathing (**Figure 2-2**).

BLS FOR CHILDREN

The following BLS techniques—rescue breathing, choking care, CPR, and use of an AED—are described for children from 1 to 8 years of age. Remember to vary your technique appropriately for infants (under age 1) or older children (over age 9 considered an adult).

Figure 2-2 Child in the recovery position.

Perform the Skill

Recovery Position

Place arm above head

Keep victim's hand under cheek to support head

1 Position the child's arm.

2 Move the child's other arm across chest and against cheek.

Roll victim over

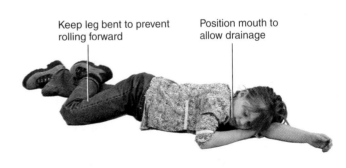

Keep leg bent to prevent rolling forward

Position mouth to allow drainage

3 Bend the child's leg and roll the child onto his or her side.

4 Adjust the child's position as needed to ensure the airway remains open.

Call First/Call Fast

If someone else is present at the scene, have that person call 911 as soon as you recognize a child is unresponsive. Shout for anyone who may hear you, and have him or her call 911 and go for an AED. If you are alone, follow these guidelines to *call first* versus *call fast* after starting to give care. In some circumstances it is important to start the process of getting an AED to the child first before starting CPR.

Because children are more sensitive to respiratory problems than adults, managing a child's airway and breathing immediately may prevent cardiac arrest. Therefore, give one minute of BLS care to a child in most cases before stopping to call 911.

Call first for:

- An infant or child with known heart problem seen to collapse suddenly

Call fast (after giving 1 minute of care) for:

- Unresponsive child or infant (0–8 years)

Rescue Breathing

Rescue breathing is used with any nonbreathing child to get needed oxygen into the lungs. Start rescue breathing immediately when you check the ABCs and discover the child is not breathing. Rescue breathing is sometimes called **artificial respiration** or **mouth-to-mouth resuscitation.**

Remember that a child who is not breathing may also be in cardiac arrest, or may soon experience cardiac arrest. Have someone call 911 immediately and, if an AED is available, send someone to get it.

Techniques of Rescue Breathing

To begin rescue breathing, position the child on his or her back and open the airway using either the head tilt-chin lift or the jaw thrust (see Chapter 1). Use a barrier device if you have one, but do not delay rescue breathing to get one. With all techniques of rescue breathing, watch the child's chest rise to make sure your air is going into the lungs.

ALERT

Rescue Breathing

Do not blow harder than is needed to make the chest rise.
After giving a breath, remember to let the air escape and watch the chest fall.
Blowing in too forcefully or for too long is ineffective and may put air in the stomach, which may cause vomiting.

Mouth-to-Barrier

Barrier devices are always recommended when giving rescue breathing. Position a pocket mask or face shield on the child's face and give breaths through the device. Make sure it is sealed to the child's face and your air is going into the child

by watching the chest rise. When using a face shield, pinch the child's nose closed when giving a breath (**Figure 2-3**).

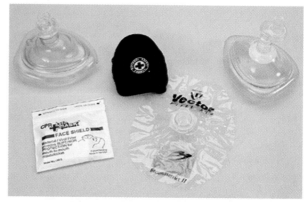

(a) Barrier devices

(b) Position pocket mask over mouth and nose

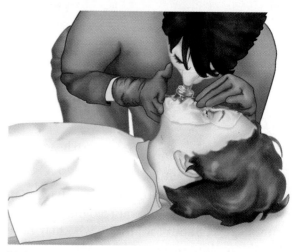

(c) Position barrier device over mouth and pinch nose

Figure 2-3 Mouth-to-barrier rescue breathing.

Perform the Skill

Rescue Breathing for Children

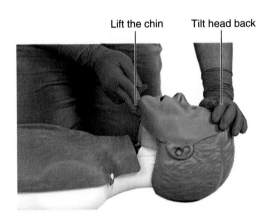

Lift the chin   Tilt head back

1 Open the airway. Look, listen, and feel for breathing for up to 10 seconds.

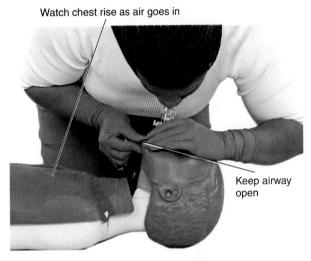

Watch chest rise as air goes in

Keep airway open

2 If not breathing give two slow breaths (1 to 1½ seconds each for a child), watching chest rise and letting it fall.

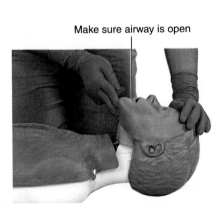

Make sure airway is open

3 If your breaths do not go in, try again to open the airway and give two more rescue breaths. If they still do not go in, the child may be choking. Proceed to CPR.

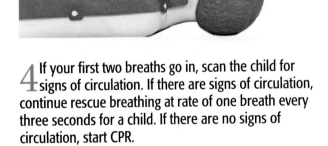

Scan for signs of breathing, movement, coughing, and normal skin condition

4 If your first two breaths go in, scan the child for signs of circulation. If there are signs of circulation, continue rescue breathing at rate of one breath every three seconds for a child. If there are no signs of circulation, start CPR.

Mouth-to-Mouth

If you do not have a barrier device, pinch the child's nose shut and seal your mouth over the child's mouth. Breathe into the child's mouth, watching the chest rise to confirm the air going in.

Mouth-to-Nose

Give rescue breathing through the child's nose if the mouth cannot be opened or is injured, or if you cannot get a good seal with your mouth over the child's. Hold the child's mouth closed, seal your mouth over the nose to breathe in, then let the mouth open to let the air escape.

Mouth-to-Stoma

Because of past illness or injury, some children breathe through a hole in their lower neck called a stoma. During your check of the ABCs check this hole to see if the child is breathing. If the child is not breathing, cup your hand over the victim's nose and mouth, seal your barrier device (or your mouth) over the stoma, and give rescue breaths as usual (**Figure 2-4**).

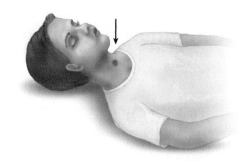

Figure 2-4 Child with a stoma.

Learning
Checkpoint (1)

1. Basic life support helps keep a child alive if _____ or _____ has stopped.

2. Rescue breathing is needed to:

   a. Get oxygen into the child's blood

   b. Circulate the blood to vital organs

   c. Open the child's airway

   d. All of the above

3. For purposes of basic life support techniques, a child is defined as someone between the ages of _____ and _____.

4. Number in correct order the links in the cardiac chain of survival:

   _____ Early defibrillation

   _____ Early access

   _____ Early CPR

   _____ Early advanced care

5. Describe the steps for putting a child in the recovery position.

_____

6. True or False: Blow as hard as you can into the child's mouth during rescue breathing.

7. What is the best way to confirm your breaths are going into the child's lungs?

   a. Listen at the child's mouth for escaping air

   b. Place one hand on the child's abdomen to feel movement

   c. Watch the child's chest rise and fall

   d. None of the above

Choking (Airway Obstruction)

Choking is a total or partial obstruction of the airway. It occurs commonly in infants and small children who put objects in their mouths and in children when eating. With a total obstruction, the child becomes unresponsive within minutes. CPR is given to an unresponsive child because the chest thrusts may expel the foreign object (see CPR section later in this chapter).

Care for Choking

When You See

In a responsive child:

- Coughing, wheezing, difficulty breathing
- Clutching at throat
- Pale or bluish coloring around mouth and nailbeds
- Acting panicked and desperate

Do This First

1. If the child is coughing, encourage continued coughing to clear the object.
2. If not coughing, ask if the child can breathe or speak. If not, give abdominal thrusts (Heimlich maneuver).
3. If the child becomes unresponsive, start CPR. If alone, call 911 after 1 minute.

Additional Care

- Continue to give abdominal thrusts until the object comes out or the child becomes unresponsive

Cardiopulmonary Resuscitation (CPR)

About four minutes after the heart stops beating, brain damage begins to occur. The more time that passes without resuscitation, the less likely it is that CPR will be successful. It is crucial to quickly recognize the need for CPR and start it immediately in a child whose heart has stopped.

CPR combines rescue breathing (to get oxygen into the victim's lungs) with chest compres-sions (to pump the oxygenated blood to vital organs). Give CPR to any victim who is not breathing and has no signs of circulation. CPR is also used for an unresponsive choking victim because the chest compressions can expel a foreign object from the victim's airway.

Remember that the specific steps for CPR vary somewhat for adults, children, and infants. The steps for children are described in the following sections.

Technique of CPR

CPR alternates giving chest compressions and rescue breaths. After checking the child's ABCs and determining there are no signs of breathing or circulation, position the child on his or her back on a flat, firm surface and start chest compressions. These are the general steps of CPR:

1. Find the correct hand position on the lower half of the breastbone midway between the nipples (**Figure 2-5**).
2. Compress the chest quickly and rhythmically with the heel of one hand at a rate of 100 compressions per minute.
3. Give cycles of five chest compressions and one rescue breath.

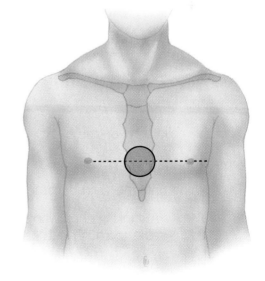

Figure 2-5 Proper hand placement for chest compressions on a child.

Perform **the Skill**

Care for Choking Children

Place hands above navel and below breastbone

1 Kneel or stand behind the child and reach around the abdomen.

2 Make a fist with one hand and grasp it with the other (thumb side into abdomen).

3 Thrust inward and upward into the abdomen with quick jerks.

4 Continue until the child can expel the object or becomes unresponsive.

5 If the child becomes unresponsive, give CPR.

Learning Checkpoint ②

1. For a responsive child who is choking:

   a. Start CPR immediately

   b. Slap the child hard on the back

   c. Give abdominal thrusts

   d. Do nothing until the child becomes unresponsive

2. True or False: A choking child who is coughing hard is still able to breathe and may be able to cough out the foreign object.

3. True or False: A choking child who is unable to breathe will soon become unresponsive and the heart will stop.

Perform the Skill
CPR for Children

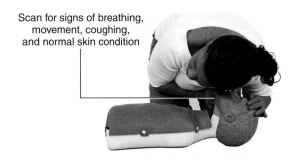

Scan for signs of breathing, movement, coughing, and normal skin condition

1 Open the airway and check for breathing for up to 10 seconds.

2 If not breathing give two rescue breaths (1 to 1$^1/_2$ seconds each).

3 Scan the victim for signs of circulation.

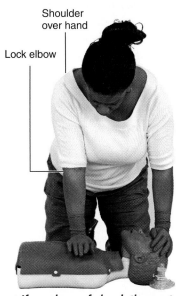

Shoulder over hand

Lock elbow

Perform finger sweep only if object is seen

4 If no signs of circulation put one hand in correct position for chest compressions.

5 Give five chest compressions 1 to 1$^1/_2$ inches deep at rate of 100 per minute. Count aloud for a steady fast rate: "One, two, three…." Then give one breath.

6 Continue cycles of five compressions and one breath. If the victim may have been choking, look inside mouth when opening the mouth to give a breath, and remove any object you see by sweeping it out with your finger.

7 After one minute of CPR, pause and check the victim again for signs of circulation. If absent, continue with chest compressions and rescue breaths. Then check again every few minutes.

8 Continue CPR until:
- The child shows signs of circulation or breathing
- An AED is brought to the scene and is ready to use
- Help arrives and takes over
- You are too exhausted to continue

9 a. If the child starts breathing and has signs of circulation, put the child in the recovery position and monitor his or her condition.
   b. If the child has signs of circulation, but is not breathing, continue giving rescue breaths at a rate of one every three seconds.
   c. If the child has no signs of circulation when AED arrives, start the AED sequence.

Chest Compressions

Be careful with your hand position for chest compressions. Do not give compressions over the bottom tip of the breastbone. When compressing, keep your elbow straight and keep your hand in contact with the chest at all times.

Compression-Only CPR

A nonbreathing child with no signs of circulation needs both rescue breathing and chest compressions to move oxygenated blood to vital organs. However, if for any reason you cannot or will not give rescue breathing, still give the child chest compressions. This gives the child a better chance for survival than doing nothing.

Automated External Defibrillators (AEDs)

Not every child who receives BLS needs an AED, but some do. Remember the chain of survival. An AED should be used with a child who is not breathing and has no signs of circulation. In cases of cardiac arrest the AED may restart a normal heartbeat.

Pediatric AED pads are available in some facilities for use by trained rescuers and first aiders. An

Learning Checkpoint ③

1. CPR stands for:

   a. Cardiac position for recovery

   b. Cardiopulmonary resuscitation

   c. Chest pump rescue

   d. None of the above

2. When is it appropriate to start CPR?

   a. As soon as you determine the child is unresponsive

   b. As soon as you determine the child is not breathing

   c. As soon as you determine the child is not breathing and has no signs of circulation

   d. Only when you have called 911 and the dispatcher instructs you to start CPR

3. Describe how to find the site for chest compressions in a child.

_____

4. Chest compressions in a child should be ___ to ___ inches deep.

5. What is the correct ratio of chest compressions to breaths in a child?

   a. 5 to 1

   b. 5 to 2

   c. 15 to 1

   d. 15 to 2

AED should never be used on an infant or child under age 8 or 55 lbs, unless it is equipped with pediatric pads. In most areas a healthcare provider oversees placement and use of the AED, and your AED training must meet certain requirements. For professional rescuers, this is called **medical direction.** Your course instructor will inform you how to meet the legal requirements in your area for using an AED.

How AEDs Work

The heart functions to pump blood to the lungs to pick up oxygen and then pump oxygenated blood to all parts of the body. The heart consists of four chambers called the left atrium, the right atrium, and the left and right ventricles. The ventricles, the lower chambers of the heart, do most of the pumping. The heart's electrical system keeps the four chambers of the heart synchronized and working together. The sinus and atrioventricular (AV) nodes help organize and control the rhythmic electrical impulses that keep the heart beating properly (**Figure 2-6**).

In some situations involving trauma, electrocution, drowning, poisoning, congenital heart disease, or other causes, the electrical system of a child's heart may be disrupted, causing an abnormal heart rhythm.

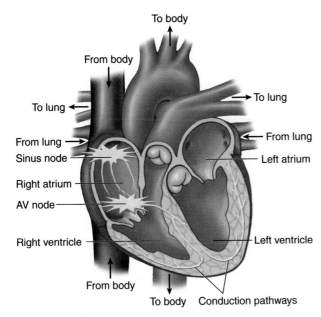

Figure 2-6 The heart.

Ventricular fibrillation (V-fib) is an abnormal heart rhythm that stops circulation of the blood. Although we say a victim in V-fib is in cardiac arrest, the heart is not actually completely still but is beating abnormally. **Fibrillation** means the ventricles of the heart are quivering instead of beating rhythmically. Blood is not filling the ventricles and is not being pumped out to the lungs or body as normal.

The AED automatically checks the child's heart rhythm and advises whether the child needs a shock. If the victim's heart is in V-fib, the unit will advise giving an electric shock to return the heart to a normal rhythm. This is called **defibrillation,** or stopping the fibrillation of the heart.

Current AEDs are easy and simple to use, but they must be used right away. With every minute that goes by before defibrillation begins, the child's chances for survival drop by about 10%.

The AED

AEDs are complex inside but simple to use. They contain a battery and are portable. The unit has two pads connected to it with cables. These pads are placed on the infant's or child's body. The unit then analyzes the victim's heart rhythm and advises whether to give a shock. Some models have a screen that tells you what to do; all models give directions in a clear voice. Different AED models vary somewhat in other features, but all work in the same basic way.

Until recently, AEDs were used only on adults because of concern that the unit could not properly analyze an infant's or child's heart rhythm and that the energy level of the shock administered by the unit was too great for the child's smaller size. New pediatric units have been approved, however, that have been shown to correctly evaluate whether the infant or child needs a shock. Special pediatric pads use an attenuator that reduces the electrical energy of the shock to a level appropriate for infants and small children. *Adult AED pads should never be used on an infant or child under age 8 or 55 lbs.* Pediatric AED pads are clearly labeled for use on infants and children (**Figure 2-7**).

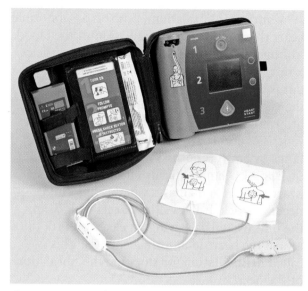

Figure 2-7 AED with pediatric electrode pads.

AED

Do not use a cell phone or 2-way
radio within 6 feet of an AED.

Using an AED

In any situation in which a child suddenly collapses or is found unresponsive, be thinking about the possibility of cardiac arrest even as you come up to the child. If someone else is present and you know an AED is available, send that person to get it *now*. It's better to have it right away and not use it than to need it and have to wait for it.

Determine the Need for an AED

As always, first check the child's ABCs. If the child is not breathing and has no signs of circulation, send someone to call 911 and to get an AED.

Start CPR

Remember the BLS steps and the chain of survival. Give CPR until the AED arrives at the scene and is ready to use. If you arrive at the scene with the AED, check the child's ABCs and then use the AED immediately before starting CPR. An easy way to remember when to use an AED is that if

you need to perform CPR on a victim, then you should also apply an AED if available.

Attach the AED

Be sure the child is not in water or in contact with metal. Water or metal conduct electricity that may pose a risk to you or others. Place the AED beside the child, turn it on, and attach the pads (electrodes) on the child's body as illustrated on the pads.

Attach the AED pads to the child only if the child is unresponsive and not breathing, and there are no signs of circulation (no movement, coughing, or breathing). Expose the child's chest, and dry the skin with a towel or dry clothing if the skin is damp. Remove the backing from the pads and apply the pads firmly on the child's body in the positions indicated by the AED manufacturer. If required with your AED model, plug the pad cables into the main unit.

Analyze and Shock

With the pads in place and the AED unit on, most AED models now automatically analyze the child's heart rhythm. Do not move or touch the child while it is analyzing. After it analyzes the heart rhythm, the unit will advise you whether to give a shock. If a shock is advised, be sure no one is touching the child. Look up and down the child and say, "Everybody clear!" Once everyone is clear, administer the shock. After the shock the AED will analyze again and advise if another shock is needed. Up to three shocks are given in this way, and then the AED will advise you to check the child and/or continue CPR. After one minute of CPR, the AED will repeat the whole process.

Note that different AEDs may use slightly different prompts. Follow the unit's words and picture prompts through this process. Some AEDs use a prompt that says "Check pulse" or something similar. As explained in Chapter 1, a pulse check should be performed only by those who have been trained to check for a pulse. Others should check instead for signs of circulation, which include breathing, coughing or crying, movement, and normal skin condition.

If signs of circulation return after any shock, check to see if the child is breathing and continue

Perform the Skill

Using an AED on an Infant or Child

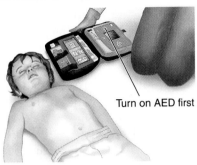

Turn on AED first

1 Position child away from water and metal.

2 Place unit beside child and turn it on.

3 Expose child's torso and dry the area if necessary.

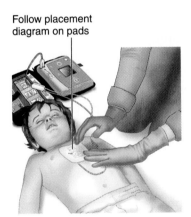

Follow placement diagram on pads

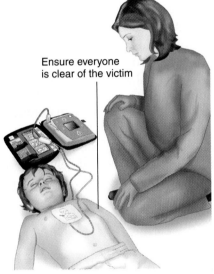

Ensure everyone is clear of the victim

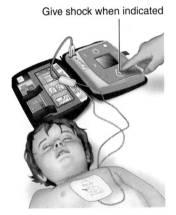

Give shock when indicated

4 Apply pads to child's torso. If needed, plug cables into unit.

5 Stay clear during rhythm analysis.

6 Follow prompts from AED unit to:
a. Press shock button *or*
b. Do not shock; check circulation, and give CPR if needed.

7 Follow prompts and your local protocol to administer sets of three shocks if needed, along with rechecking signs of circulation and giving CPR as needed.

8 If the child regains signs of circulation and is breathing, put in recovery position and monitor ABCs.

to provide rescue breathing if necessary. Put an unresponsive, breathing child in the recovery position and continue to monitor the ABCs. Keep the AED pads in place as some children may return to V-fib and require defibrillation again.

The AED may also say no shock is indicated. This means the child's heart will not benefit from defibrillation. If so, check the child's ABCs again and give CPR if there are no signs of circulation.

Special Situations

Some situations involve special considerations in the use of the AED.

Injured Victims

Cardiac arrest in a severely injured child is usually caused by the traumatic injury, not by a heart rhythm problem like V-fib. In such cases your local medical direction may specify not to use the AED. However, if the injury seems minor, the child's cardiac arrest may respond to defibrillation. You should attach the pads and follow the prompts from the AED.

Hypothermia Victims

Determining signs of circulation in a victim of hypothermia (low body temperature) can be difficult. Handle a hypothermic child very carefully because jarring may cause cardiac arrest. Follow your local guidelines for AED use if you find no signs of circulation. Typically, if the AED finds a shockable rhythm and advises shocks, only a total of three are given, and then CPR is performed until help arrives. Note that a victim of hypothermia can often be resuscitated even after a prolonged period of time. In this case always attempt resuscitation even if a long time has elapsed.

Potential AED Problems

An AED must be maintained regularly and the battery kept charged (see "AED Maintenance" section). With regular maintenance an AED should not have any problems during use.

The AED may also prompt you to avoid problems. If you get a low battery prompt, change the battery before continuing. Another prompt may advise you to prevent moving the child, if the AED detects motion.

AED Maintenance

AEDs require regular maintenance. Check the manual from the manufacturer for periodic scheduled maintenance and testing of the unit. A daily inspection of the unit helps ensure the AED is always ready for use and all needed supplies are present. Professional rescuers usually inspect the unit at the beginning of their shift. Most facilities with an AED use a daily checklist form. A checklist should always be adapted for the specific AED model, including the manufacturer's daily maintenance guidelines. In addition, many units come with a simulator device to be used to check that the AED is correctly analyzing rhythms and delivering shocks; this may be part of the daily inspection routine (**Figure 2-8**).

Learning
Checkpoint (4)

1. True or False: An AED works by giving a shock to a heart that is fibrillating to restore it to a normal rhythm.

2. True or False: It is very risky to use an AED because the unit cannot tell whether the child's heart is beating normally or not.

3. Which statement is true about the electrode pads of an AED?

  a. The AED has two pads which must be correctly positioned

  b. The AED has four pads which must be correctly positioned

  c. The AED has two pads, but only one needs to be put on the child (the other is a spare)

  d. The pads are used only if a heart rhythm is not detected when the machine is placed in the center of the victim's chest

4. If the AED unit advises you to give a shock, what do you do next?

   a. Continue CPR while asking someone else to push the shock button

   b. Place a wet towel over the child's chest and push the shock button

   c. Make sure everyone is clear of the child and then push the shock button

   d. Press down on the electrode pad and push the shock button

5. An AED will usually advise giving a series of up to _____ shocks before advising you to stop and check for signs of circulation or give CPR.

6. Name at least one situation in which a young child may experience sudden cardiac arrest and could benefit from use of an AED: _____

AED INSPECTION CHECKLIST

Date: _____ Location: _____ AED Model: _____

Inspected by: _____ Signed: _____

Criteria	ok/no	Corrective action/remarks
AED unit		
verify correctly placed	——	_____
clean, clear of objects	——	_____
no cracks or damage to case	——	_____
cables/connectors present and not expired	——	_____
fully charged battery in place	——	_____
charged spare battery present	——	_____
check status/service light indicator	——	_____
check absence of service alarm	——	_____
power on, self-test	——	_____
Supplies	——	
Two sealed sets of electrode pads		
Verify expiration date on pad packages	——	_____
Medical exam gloves	——	_____
Hand towels	——	_____
Alcohol wipes	——	_____
Scissors	——	_____
Pocket mask or face shield	——	_____

Figure 2-8 Example of an AED checklist.

Perform the Skill

Rescue Breathing for Infants

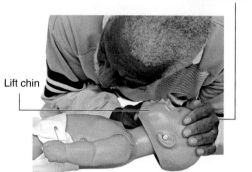

Tilt head back

Lift chin

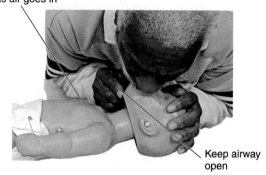

Watch chest rise as air goes in

Keep airway open

1 Open the airway. Look, listen, and feel for breathing for up to 10 seconds.

2 If not breathing, give two slow breaths (1 to 1½ seconds each), watching chest rise and letting it fall.

Make sure airway is open

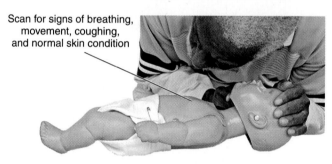

Scan for signs of breathing, movement, coughing, and normal skin condition

3 If your breaths do not go in, try again to open the airway and give two more rescue breaths. If they still do not go in, the infant may be choking. Proceed to CPR.

4 If your first two breaths go in, scan for signs of circulation. If there are signs of circulation, continue rescue breathing at rate of one breath every 3 seconds. If there are no signs of circulation, start CPR.

BLS FOR INFANTS

BLS techniques for infants (under age 1) are similar to those used for children (age 1 to 8). The differences are described in the following sections.

Call First/Call Fast for Infants

If someone else is present at the scene, have that person call 911 as soon as you recognize an infant is unresponsive. Shout for anyone who may hear you, and have him or her call 911. If you are alone, follow these guidelines to *call first* versus *call fast* after starting to give care. In some circumstances it is important to start the process of getting advanced medical help for the infant before starting CPR.

Call first for:

- An infant or child with known heart problem seen to collapse suddenly

Call fast (after giving 1 minute of CPR) for:

- Unresponsive child or infant (0–8 years)

Rescue Breathing

Rescue breathing for infants is similar to that for children, with these differences:

- Gently tilt the head back to open the airway and check breathing—do not overextend the neck

Perform the Skill

Choking in an Infant

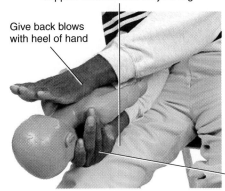

Support infant's torso on your leg

Give back blows with heel of hand

Support infant's head and neck

1 Support the infant's head in one hand, with the torso on your forearm on your thigh. Give up to five back blows between the shoulder blades.

2 Check mouth for expelled object. If object not expelled, continue with next step.

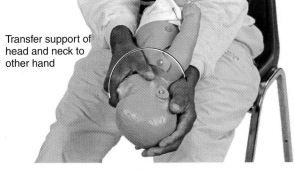

Transfer support of head and neck to other hand

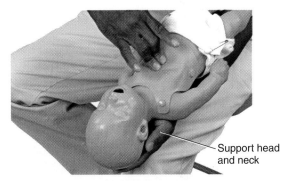

Support head and neck

3 With other hand on back of infant's head, roll the infant face up.

4 Give up to five chest thrusts with middle and ring fingers. Check mouth for expelled object.

5 Repeat steps 1 to 4, alternating back blows and chest thrusts and checking the mouth. If alone, call 911 after one minute. Continue until object is expelled or infant becomes unresponsive.

6 If the infant becomes unresponsive, give CPR.

- Cover both the mouth and nose with your mouth to give breaths (use the mouth or nose only if you cannot cover both)
- Give breaths in shallow puffs of air lasting 1 to 1½ seconds each

Choking (Airway Obstruction)

Choking care for infants is somewhat different from that for children. If a choking infant is crying or coughing, watch carefully to see if the object comes out. If a choking responsive infant is not crying or coughing, assume the airway is obstructed. Rather than abdominal thrusts as with a child, an infant is given alternating back blows and chest thrusts.

If a choking infant becomes unresponsive, send someone to call 911, and start CPR. Check for an object in the mouth each time before you give a breath, and sweep out any object you see with one finger.

Cardiopulmonary Resuscitation (CPR)

CPR serves the same purposes for infants as for children: to provide oxygen and to circulate the blood to vital organs. The technique, however, is somewhat different.

Technique of CPR

After checking the infant's ABCs and determining there are no signs of breathing or circulation, start chest compressions. These are the general steps of CPR for an infant:

1. Find the correct compression position. Use two fingers on the lower half of the breastbone just below a line between the nipples (**Figure 2-9**).

2. Compress the chest quickly and rhythmically at a rate of at least 100 compressions per minute.

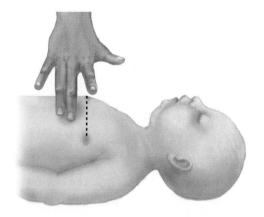

Figure 2-9 Proper hand placement for chest compressions on an infant.

3. Give cycles of five chest compressions and one rescue breath.

Basic Life Support

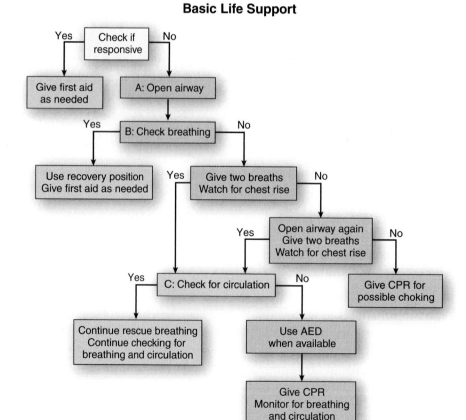

Figure 2-10 BLS flowchart.

Learning
Checkpoint (5)

1. How long do you blow into the infant when giving rescue breathing?

   a. ½ second

   b. ½ to 1 second

   c. 1 to 1½ seconds

   d. 1½ to 2 seconds

2. If the infant has signs of circulation but is not breathing, continue to give rescue breaths at a rate of 1 breath every ____ seconds.

3. For a responsive choking infant:

   a. Support the head as you position the infant

   b. Alternate back blows and chest thrusts

   c. Check the infant's mouth for an expelled object

   d. All of the above

4. Explain why CPR is given to a choking infant who becomes unresponsive.

   _____

5. Which is the correct way to give chest compressions to an infant?

   a. With one hand on top of the other on the infant's chest

   b. With the heel of one hand only

   c. With middle two fingers

   d. Any of these are acceptable

6. CPR is given to an infant in cycles of ____ compression(s) followed by ____ breath(s).

Perform the Skill
CPR for Infants

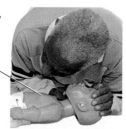

Scan for signs of breathing, movement, coughing, and normal skin condition

1 Open the airway and check for breathing for up to 10 seconds.

2 If not breathing give two rescue breaths (1 to 1½ seconds each).

3 Scan the infant for signs of circulation.

Keep airway open

Perform finger sweep only if object is seen

4 If no signs of circulation, put your two middle fingers about one finger-width below an imaginary line between the nipples for chest compressions.

5 Give five chest compressions ½ to 1 inch deep at rate of at least 100 per minute. Count aloud for a steady fast rate: "One, two, three…." Then give another breath.

6 Continue cycles of five compressions followed by one breath. If the infant may have been choking, look inside the mouth before giving rescue breaths.

7 After one minute of CPR, pause and check the infant again for signs of circulation, then continue with chest compressions and rescue breaths. Check again every few minutes.

8 Continue CPR until:
- Infant shows signs of circulation or breathing
- Help arrives and takes over
- You are too exhausted to continue

9 a. If the infant starts breathing and has signs of circulation, hold the infant and continue to monitor his or her condition.
b. If the infant has signs of circulation but is not breathing, continue giving rescue breaths at a rate of one every 3 seconds.

Automated External Defibrillators (AEDs)

Pediatric AED electrode pads can be used on infants in cardiac arrest as well as on children under age 8. The technique is the same as that described for children.

Summary of Basic Life Support

Step	Infant (under 1 year)	Child (1–8 years)	Adult (over 8 years)
1. Check for responsiveness	Stimulate to check response	"Are you okay" Tap shoulder	"Are you okay" Tap shoulder
2. If unresponsive, call 911	Send someone to call Give 1 minute of care before calling yourself if alone	Send someone to call Give 1 minute of care before calling yourself if alone (except for known heart problem)	Send someone to call Call immediately if alone (give 1 minute of CPR for victim of drowning, poisoning, injury)
3. If unresponsive: Open airway	Head tilt-chin lift (but do not overextend neck)	Head tilt-chin lift or jaw thrust	Head tilt-chin lift or jaw thrust
4. Check breathing	Look, listen, feel for breathing	Look, listen, feel for breathing	Look, listen, feel for breathing
5. If not breathing: Give 2 breaths, watch chest rise	Use barrier device or cover mouth/nose or nose Each breath lasts 1 to 1½ seconds	Use barrier device or cover mouth, nose, or stoma Each breath lasts 1 to 1½ seconds	Use barrier device or cover mouth, nose, or stoma Each breath lasts 2 seconds
6. If chest does not rise: Reposition airway and try 2 breaths again	Each breath lasts 1 to 1½ seconds	Each breath lasts 1 to 1½ seconds	Each breath lasts 2 seconds
7. If chest still does not rise: Start CPR for airway obstruction (choking care)	For compressions use 2 fingers one finger-width below line between nipples Compress chest ½–1 inch Compress at rate of at least 100/minute 5 compressions per 1 breath	For compressions use one hand midway between nipples Compress chest 1–1½ inches Compress at rate of 100/minute 5 compressions per 1 breath	For compressions use both hands, one on top of other, midway between nipples Compress chest 1½–2 inches Compress at rate of 100/minute 15 compressions per 2 breaths

(continued)

Step	Infant (under 1 year)	Child (1–8 years)	Adult (over 8 years)
8. Check for signs of circulation	Scan body for movement, breathing, coughing, and normal skin condition	Scan body for movement, breathing, coughing, and normal skin condition	Scan body for movement, breathing, coughing, and normal skin condition
9. If circulation signs present but no breathing, give rescue breathing	1 breath every 3 seconds	1 breath every 3 seconds	1 breath every 5 seconds
10. If no signs of circulation present, give CPR (unless AED is present)	Cycles of 5 compressions and 1 breath	Cycles of 5 compressions and 1 breath	Cycles of 15 compressions and 2 breaths
11. Continue to check for breathing and signs of circulation	Look, listen, and feel for breathing and scan body for signs of circulation	Look, listen, and feel for breathing and scan body for signs of circulation	Look, listen, and feel for breathing and scan body for signs of circulation
12. Use AED when available (if no breathing or signs of circulation)	Use only pediatric electrode pads	Use only pediatric electrode pads	Use adult AED electrode pads
13. If victim recovers breathing and signs of circulation, put in recovery position	Hold infant and monitor ABCs	Lay on side in recovery position and monitor ABCs	Lay on side in recovery position and monitor ABCs

3 Bleeding and Wound Care

Many injuries cause external or internal bleeding. Bleeding may be minor or life threatening. In addition to knowing how to control bleeding in a child, you should know how to care for different kinds of wounds and how to apply dressings and bandages.

TYPES OF EXTERNAL BLEEDING

There are three types of external bleeding (**Figure 3-1**):

- **Bleeding from injured arteries** is generally more serious and is more likely with deep injuries. The blood is bright red, and may spurt from the wound, and blood loss can be very rapid. This bleeding needs to be controlled immediately.
- **Bleeding from injured veins** is generally slower and steady but can still be serious. The blood is dark red and flows steadily rather than spurting. This bleeding is usually easier to control.
- **Bleeding from capillaries** occurs with shallow cuts or scrapes and often stops soon by itself. The wound still needs attention to prevent infection.

CONTROLLING EXTERNAL BLEEDING

For minor bleeding, clean and dress the wound (as described later). Usually the bleeding stops by itself or with light pressure on the dressing. For more serious bleeding, give first aid *immediately* to stop the bleeding.

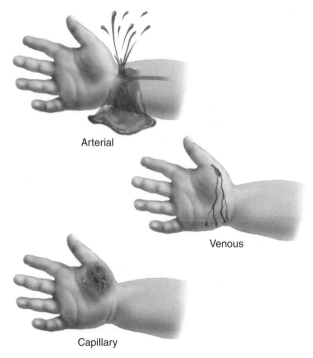

Arterial

Venous

Capillary

Figure 3-1 Types of external bleeding.

When You See

- Bleeding from a wound
- Blood on a child
- Signs of shock (see Chapter 4)

Do This First

1. Put on medical exam gloves or use another barrier to protect yourself from contact with the blood (such as dressings, a plastic bag, or the child's own hand).
2. Move aside any clothing and place a sterile dressing (or clean cloth) on the wound, then apply direct pressure on the wound with your hand.
3. With a bleeding arm or leg, raise the limb above the heart level while keeping pressure on the wound. Be careful moving the child because of the possibility of other injuries.
4. If blood soaks through the dressing, do not remove the old dressing but put another dressing or cloth pad on top of it and keep applying pressure.

5. If possible, wrap a roller bandage around the limb to hold the dressings in place and apply pressure. Be careful not to cut off circulation to the limb with the many wraps of a roller bandage around the child's small limb.
6. If direct pressure does not control the bleeding, also apply indirect pressure at a pressure point in the arm or leg to squeeze the artery closed (Figure 3-2).

Additional Care

- Call 911
- Treat the child for shock if necessary (see Chapter 4)
- Do not remove the dressings/bandage. The wound will be cleaned later by medical personnel
- Keep the child calm and distracted to ensure cooperation

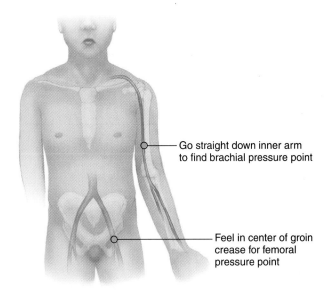

Go straight down inner arm to find brachial pressure point

Feel in center of groin crease for femoral pressure point

Figure 3-2 Indirect pressure points.

Bleeding

Use your bare hands only if no barrier is available, and then wash immediately.
Do not put pressure on an object in a wound.
Do not put pressure on the scalp if the skull may be injured.
Do not use a tourniquet to stop bleeding except as an extreme last resort (limb will likely be lost).

Perform the Skill

Controlling Bleeding

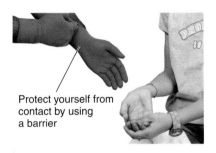

Protect yourself from contact by using a barrier

1 Put on gloves.

Apply pressure directly on wound

2 Place a sterile dressing on the wound and apply direct pressure with your hand.

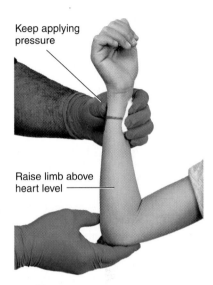

Keep applying pressure

Raise limb above heart level

3 Elevate a bleeding arm or leg to help slow the bleeding.

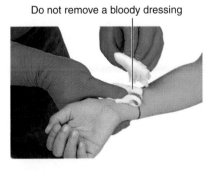

Do not remove a bloody dressing

4 If needed, put another dressing or cloth pad on top of the first and keep applying pressure.

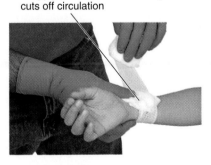

Make sure bandage is tight enough to apply pressure but not so tight it cuts off circulation

5 Apply a roller bandage to keep pressure on the wound.

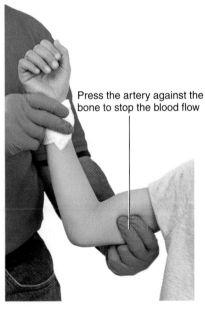

Press the artery against the bone to stop the blood flow

6 If needed, apply pressure at pressure point.

Learning
Checkpoint ①

1. True or False: Arterial bleeding is the most serious because blood loss can be very rapid.

2. True or False: The first thing to do with any bleeding wound is wash it and apply antibiotic ointment.

3. Number the steps for bleeding control in correct order:

_____ Use indirect pressure

_____ Put direct pressure on wound using a dressing

_____ Put on gloves

_____ Apply additional dressings

_____ Apply pressure bandage

_____ Elevate the limb

4. If you do not have medical exam gloves with you, what other materials or objects can be used as a barrier between your hand and the wound when applying direct pressure?

_____

5. When should a tourniquet be used?

_____

WOUND CARE

Wound care involves cleaning and dressing a wound to prevent infection and protect the wound so that healing can occur. Remember: *Do not waste time cleaning a wound that is severely bleeding. Controlling the bleeding is the priority.* Healthcare personnel will clean the wound as needed.

The main types of open wounds include the following:

• **Abrasions** occur when the top skin is scraped off. Foreign material may be present in the wound that can cause infection (**Figure 3-3**).

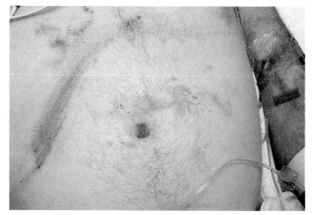

Figure 3-3 Abrasion.

- **Lacerations**, or cuts, may be straight-edged (incision) or jagged, and may cause heavy bleeding (Figure 3-4).
- **Punctures** of the skin are caused by a sharp object penetrating down into the skin and possibly deeper tissues and are more likely to trap foreign material in the body (Figure 3-5).
- **Avulsions** are areas of skin or other tissue torn partially from the body, like a flap (Figure 3-6).

Other special wounds are described in the following pages.

Cleaning Wounds

Unless the wound is very large or bleeding seriously, or the child has other injuries needing attention, clean the wound to help prevent infection. Wash your hands first and wear gloves if available.

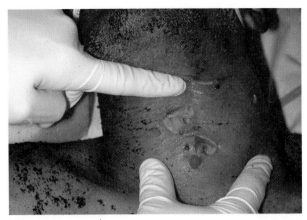
Figure 3-4 Laceration.

When You See

- An open wound

Do This First

1. Gently wash the wound with soap and water and a gauze pad or clean washcloth to remove dirt.
2 Use the gauze pad or tweezers to remove any small particles.
3. Pat the area dry. With abrasions only, apply an antibiotic ointment (follow your childcare center's policy).
4. Cover the wound with a sterile dressing and bandage (or adhesive bandage with nonstick pad).

Additional Care

- If stitches may be needed (see later section), or if the child does not have a current tetanus vaccination, seek medical attention
- Change the dressing daily or if it becomes wet. (If a dressing sticks to the wound, soak it in water first.) Advise the child's parents or caretakers to seek medical attention if the wound later looks infected
- Keep the child calm and distracted to ensure cooperation

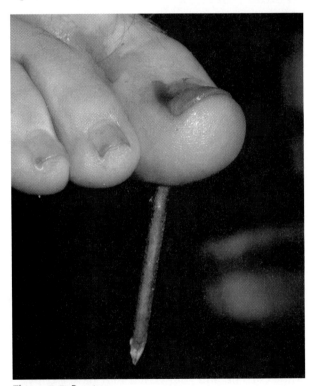
Figure 3-5 Puncture.

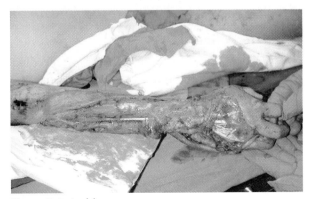
Figure 3-6 Avulsion.

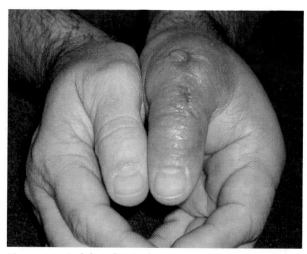

Figure 3-7 An infected wound.

Wound Infection

Any wound can become infected. The child then needs medical attention. The signs and symptoms of a wound infection include the following (**Figure 3-7**):

- Wound area is red, swollen, and warm
- Pain
- Pus
- Fever
- Red streaks or trails on the skin near the wound are a sign the infection is spreading—see a healthcare provider immediately

Seek medical attention for any deep or puncture wound. With any deep or puncture wound, the risk of tetanus—a very serious infection—must be considered. Children are recommended to receive a series of tetanus vaccinations when young, followed by a booster in early adolescence and at least every 10 years thereafter. Some childcare centers and schools require children's vaccinations to be current, and your center may have a copy of this record. Parents or guardians should be advised when a tetanus shot may be needed.

Dressing Wounds

Dressings are put on wounds to help stop bleeding, prevent infection, and protect the wound while healing. First aid kits should include sealed sterile gauze dressings in many sizes. Adhesive strips such as Band-Aids® are dressings combined with a bandage. If a sterile dressing is not available, use a clean, nonfluffy cloth as a dressing (**Figure 3-8**).

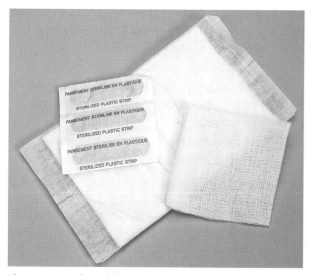

Figure 3-8 Variety of dressings.

After washing and drying the wound, apply the dressing this way:

1. Wash your hands and wear gloves.
2. Choose a dressing larger than the wound.
3. Carefully lay the dressing on the wound (do not slide it on from the side).
4. If blood seeps through, do not remove the dressing but add more dressings on top.
5. Apply a bandage to hold the dressing in place (see later section on bandaging).

When to Seek Medical Attention

Remember to call 911 for severe bleeding. In addition, a child should see a healthcare provider as soon as possible in these situations:

- Bleeding is not easily controlled
- Any deep or large wound
- Significant wounds on the face
- Signs and symptoms that the wound is infected
- Any bite from an animal or human
- Foreign object or material embedded in the wound
- Any uncertainty about the child's tetanus vaccination
- The child may need stitches within hours for:
  - Cuts on the face or hands when the edges do not close together
  - Gaping wounds
  - Cuts longer than 1 inch

Learning Checkpoint 2

1. Check off the actions below to include in wound care:

_____ Wash minor wounds with soap and water

_____ Pour rubbing alcohol on any wound

_____ Wash major wounds to help stop the bleeding

_____ Use tweezers to remove dirt particles from a minor wound

_____ Cover any wound with a sterile dressing and bandage

_____ Let a scab form before washing a minor wound

_____ See a healthcare provider for a deep or puncture wound

_____ Blow on a minor wound to cool the area and relieve pain

2. If you are changing a wound dressing a day after the injury and the dressing sticks to the wound, what should you do?

_____

3. True or False: Puncture wounds have little risk for infection.

4. True or False: You don't need to bother putting on gloves to dress a minor wound if you know the child well.

5. For what type of wound may an antibiotic ointment be appropriate?

_____

6. Check off which signs and symptoms may indicate a wound is infected:

_____ Headache

_____ Red, swollen area

_____ Cool, clammy skin

_____ Nausea and vomiting

_____ Warmth in the area

_____ Fever

_____ A scab forms that looks dark brown

_____ Pus drains from the wound

7. Which of these children need to seek medical attention? (Check all that apply.)

_____ Jose has a deep laceration on his hand from a sharp-edged toy, but you managed to stop the bleeding in 15 minutes.

_____ While playing in the park Rebecca was bitten by a squirrel, but the bleeding stopped almost immediately.

_____ Carl scraped his knee when he fell off his bicycle, but the abrasion washed out clean and you have applied an antibiotic ointment (following your childcare center's policy).

_____ Kim got a bad gash on her cheek from playground equipment, but she had already stopped the bleeding with her hand by the time you saw her.

Special Wounds

Puncture Wounds

Puncture wounds have a greater risk of infection because often they bleed less and therefore germs may not be flushed out. In addition to routine wound care, take the following steps:

1. Remove any small objects or dirt but not larger impaled objects (see next section).
2. Gently press on wound edges to promote bleeding.
3. Do not put any medication inside or over the puncture wound.
4. Wash the wound well with running water directed at the puncture site.
5. Dress the wound and seek medical attention.

Impaled Objects

Removing an object from a wound could cause more injury and bleeding. Leave it in place and dress the wound around it.

1. Control bleeding by applying direct pressure at the sides of the object. If in an arm or leg, raise the area above the level of the heart.
2. Dress the wound around the object.
3. Pad the object in place with large dressings or folded cloths.
4. Support the object while bandaging it in place.
5. Seek medical attention.

Amputation

In an amputation injury a body part has been severed from the body. Control the bleeding and care for the wound first. Call 911 and give care for shock as needed. Then recover and care for the amputated part. Use the following steps:

1. Wrap the severed part in dry sterile gauze. Do not wash it.
2. Place the part in a plastic bag and seal it.
3. Place the sealed bag in another bag or container with ice. Do not let the part touch ice directly, and do not surround it with ice (**Figure 3-9**).
4. Make sure the severed part is given to the responding crew or taken with the child to the emergency room.

Figure 3-9   Keep amputated part cold but not directly touching ice.

Genital Injuries

Provide privacy for a child with bleeding or injury in the genital area. Follow these guidelines:

- Use direct pressure to control external bleeding
- For injured testicles, provide support with a towel between the legs like a diaper
- Call 911 for severe or continuing bleeding or significant pain or swelling. See Chapter 12 for steps to take if you suspect the possibility of sexual abuse

Head and Face Wounds

Injuries to a child's head or face may require special first aid. The following sections list guidelines for these special injuries.

With any significant injury to the head, the child may also have a neck or spinal injury (see Chapter 6). If you suspect a spinal injury, be careful not to move the child's head while giving first aid for head and face wounds.

Skull Injuries

If the child is bleeding from the scalp, consider the additional possibility of a skull fracture if the child had a blow to the head.

When You See

- A deformed area of the skull
- A depressed area in the bone felt during the physical examination

- Blood or fluid from the ears or nose
- Object impaled in the skull

Do This First

1. If the child is unresponsive, check the ABCs.
2. Do not clean the wound, press on it, or remove an impaled object.
3. Cover the wound with a sterile dressing.
4. If there is significant bleeding, apply pressure only around the edges of the wound, not on the wound itself.
5. Do not move the child unnecessarily, since there may also be a spinal injury.

Additional Care

- Call 911 and stay with the child
- Put an unresponsive child who is breathing in the recovery position (unless there may be a spinal injury)
- Seek medical attention if the child later experiences nausea and vomiting, persistent headache, drowsiness or disorientation, stumbling or lack of coordination, or problems with speech or vision
- Keep the child calm and distracted to ensure cooperation

Head Wounds Without Suspected Skull Fracture

When You See

- Bleeding from the head
- No sign of skull fracture

Do This First

1. Replace any skin flaps and cover the wound with a sterile dressing.
2. Use direct pressure to control bleeding.
3. Put a roller or triangle bandage around the child's head to secure the dressing (**Figure 3-10**).

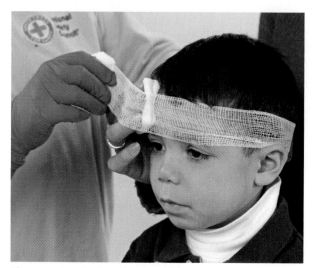

Figure 3-10 Dressing a head wound.

Figure 3-11 Blow to eye.

Additional Care

- Position the child with head and shoulders raised to help control bleeding
- If the wound was caused by a blow to the head or the wound may require stitches, the child should see a healthcare provider
- Keep the child calm and distracted to ensure cooperation

Eye Injuries

Eye injuries can be serious because vision may be affected.

For a blow to the eye:

1. If the eye is bleeding or leaking fluid, call 911 immediately. Cover the injured eye with a paper cup bandaged or taped in place.
2. If the eye is not bleeding or leaking fluid, put a cold pack over the eye for 15 minutes to ease pain and reduce swelling, but do not put pressure on the eye (**Figure 3-11**). If the child is wearing a contact lens, do not remove it.
3. Have the child lie still and also cover the uninjured eye. Movement of the uninjured eye causes movement of the injured one.
4. Seek medical attention if pain persists or vision is affected in any way.

For a large object embedded in the eye:

1. Do not remove the object. Stabilize it in place with dressings or bulky cloth.
2. Cover both eyes because movement of the uninjured one causes movement of the injured one.
3. Call 911 immediately.

For dirt or a small particle in the eye:

1. Do not let the child rub the eye.
2. Gently pull the upper eyelid out and down over the lower eyelid.
3. If the particle remains, gently flush the eye with water from a medicine dropper or water glass. Have the child hold his or her head with the affected eye lower than the other so that water does not flow into the unaffected eye.
4. If the particle remains and is visible, carefully try to remove it with a sterile dressing. Lift the upper eyelid and swab its underside if you see the particle (**Figure 3-12**).
5. If the particle still remains or the child has any vision problems or pain, cover the eye with a sterile dressing and seek medical attention. Also cover the uninjured eye,

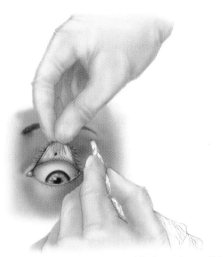

Figure 3-12 Carefully remove a particle from the eyelid.

because movement of the uninjured eye causes movement of the injured one.

For a chemical or substance splashed in the eye:

1. Rinse the eye with running water for 20 minutes. Have the child hold his or her head with the affected eye lower than the other so that water does not flow into the unaffected eye (see Chapter 5).
2. Call the Poison Control Center to determine what medical care may be needed.

Ear Injuries

With bleeding from the external ear, control the bleeding with direct pressure and dress the wound. For bleeding from within the ear, follow these guidelines:

When You See

- Bleeding inside the ear
- Signs of pain
- Possible deafness

Do This First

1. If the blood looks watery (which could mean a skull fracture) or the bleeding results from a blow to the head, call 911.

2. Help the child to sit up, tilting the affected ear lower to let blood drain out.
3. Cover the ear with a loose sterile dressing, but do not apply pressure.
4. Seek medical attention immediately.

Additional Care

- Keep the ear covered to reduce the risk of infection
- Keep the child calm and distracted to ensure cooperation

ALERT

Ear Wound

Do not plug the ear closed to try to stop bleeding.

Nosebleed

A nosebleed can be alarming because it often occurs suddenly and may seem to bleed heavily.

When You See

- Blood coming from either or both nostrils
- Blood possibly running from back of nose down into the mouth or throat

Do This First

1. Have the child sit and tilt his or her head slightly forward with the mouth open. Carefully remove any object you see in the nose.
2. Wearing gloves, pinch the child's nostrils together just below the bridge of the nose and hold for 10 minutes; an older child may be able to hold his or her nostrils pinched closed. Ask the child to breathe through the mouth and not speak, swallow, cough, or sniff.
3. If the child is gasping or choking on blood in the throat, call 911.
4. After 10 minutes, release the pressure slowly. Pinch the nostrils again for another 10 minutes if bleeding continues.

Figure 3-13 Nosebleed care.

5. Place a cold compress on the bridge of the nose (**Figure 3-13**).

Additional Care

- Seek medical attention if:
  - bleeding continues after two attempts to control bleeding
  - you suspect the nose is broken
  - the child is known to have high blood pressure
- Have the child rest for a few hours and avoid rubbing, picking at, or blowing the nose
- Keep the child calm and distracted to ensure cooperation

ALERT

Nosebleed
Do not tilt the child's head backward.
Do not have the child lie down.

Broken Nose

When You See

- Obvious deformity of the nose

- Swelling
- Blood coming from either or both nostrils

Do This First

1. Have the child sit and tilt his or her head slightly forward with the mouth open.
2. If bleeding is significant, try to stop the bleeding by pinching the nostrils closed as for a nosebleed.
3. Call 911 or seek medical attention.

Mouth and Tooth Injuries

For a tooth knocked out:

1. Have the child sit with head tilted forward to let blood drain out.
2. To control bleeding, fold or roll gauze into a pad and place it over the tooth socket. Have the child bite down to put pressure on the pad for 20 to 30 minutes (**Figure 3-14**).
3. Save the tooth, which may be reimplanted if the child sees a dentist within the first hour after the injury. Touching only the tooth's crown, rinse it if dirty and replace it in its socket if possible; hold it in place with gauze a pad. Otherwise, put it in a container of milk, the child's saliva, or cool water. (Saline solution may also be used if available.)

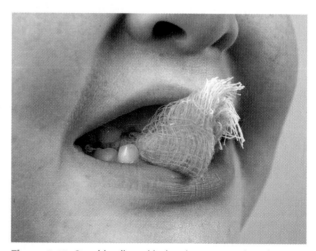

Figure 3-14 Stop bleeding with dressing over tooth socket.

4. Get the child and the tooth to a dentist immediately. (Most dentists have 24-hour emergency call numbers.)

For other bleeding in the mouth:

1. Have the child sit with head tilted forward to let blood drain out.

2. For a wound penetrating the lip: Put a rolled dressing between the lip and the gum. Hold a second dressing against the outside lip.

3. For a bleeding tongue: Put a dressing on the wound and apply pressure.

4. Do not rinse the mouth (this may prevent clotting).

5. Do not let the child swallow blood, which may cause vomiting.

6. Do not let the child drink anything warm for several hours.

7. Seek medical attention if bleeding is severe or does not stop.

BANDAGES

Bandages are used for covering a dressing, keeping the dressing on a wound, and applying pressure to stop bleeding. Because only dressings touch the wound itself, bandages need to be clean but not necessarily sterile. As described in Chapter 7, bandages are also used to support or immobilize an injury to bones, joints, or muscles and to reduce swelling.

Learning
Checkpoint ③

1. Name one circumstance in which you might want to promote bleeding.

_____

2. True or False: The first thing to do when you see an object impaled in a wound is to pull it out so that you can put direct pressure on the wound to stop the bleeding.

3. True or False: An amputated part should be kept cold but not put in direct contact with ice.

4. List two or three signs of a possible skull fracture. What is one thing you should not do to stop bleeding from the head if you suspect a skull fracture?

_____

5. With an eye injury, why should you cover the _uninjured_ eye too?

_____

6. Describe three ways you can try to remove a small particle from the eye.

_____

7. True or False: For bleeding from within the ear, roll a piece of gauze into a plug and try to seal the ear with it.

8. For a child with a nosebleed, first try to stop the bleeding by pinching the nostrils closed for _____ minutes. During this time, list two or three things the child should **not do.**

_____

9. True or False: A knocked-out tooth can be reimplanted if it is kept wet and the child reaches a dentist within an hour.

10. True or False: Repeatedly rinsing the mouth with cool water is the best way to stop bleeding in the mouth.

Types of Bandages

Your first aid kit should contain a variety of bandages. All the following are examples of bandages (**Figure 3-15**):

- Adhesive compresses or strips for small wounds that combine a dressing with an adhesive bandage
- Adhesive tape rolls (cloth, plastic, paper)
- Tubular bandages for finger or toe
- Elastic bandages
- Cloth roller bandages
- Triangular bandages (or folded square cloths)
- Any cloth or other material improvised to meet purposes of bandaging

Guidelines for Bandaging

1. To put pressure on a wound to stop bleeding or to prevent swelling of an injury, apply the bandage firmly—but not so tightly that it cuts off circulation. With a bandage around a limb, check the fingers or toes for color, warmth, and sensation (normal touch, not tingling) to make sure circulation is not cut off. If there are signs of reduced circulation, unwrap the bandage and reapply it less tightly.
2. Since swelling continues after many injuries, keep checking the tightness of the bandage. Swelling may make a loose bandage tight enough to cut off circulation.
3. With a bandaged wound, be sure the bandage is secure enough that the dressing will not move and expose the wound to possible contamination.
4. With elastic and roller bandages, anchor the first end and tie, tape, or pin the ending section in place.

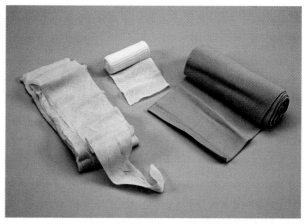

Figure 3-15 Types of bandages.

5. Use a nonelastic roller bandage to make a circular pressure bandage around a limb to control bleeding and protect the wound.
6. An elastic roller bandage is used to support a joint and prevent swelling. At the wrist or ankle a figure-eight wrap is used.

INTERNAL BLEEDING

Internal bleeding is any bleeding within the body in which the blood does not escape from an open wound. A closed wound may have minor local bleeding in the skin and other superficial tissue, causing a bruise. A more serious injury of the torso can cause deeper organs to bleed severely. This bleeding, although unseen, can be life threatening. (See also Chapter 6 on closed abdominal wounds.)

Internal Bleeding

Do not give the child anything to drink even if he or she is very thirsty.

Perform the Skill

Applying a Circular Pressure Bandage

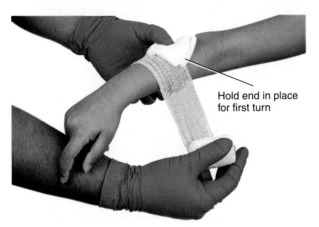

Hold end in place
for first turn

1 Anchor the starting end of the bandage below the wound dressing.

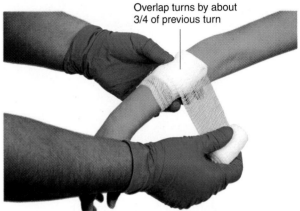

Overlap turns by about
3/4 of previous turn

2 Make several circular turns, then overlap turns.

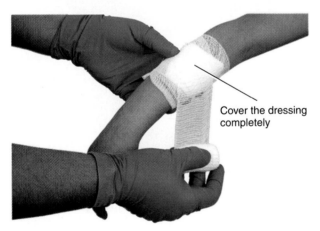

Cover the dressing
completely

3 Work up the limb.

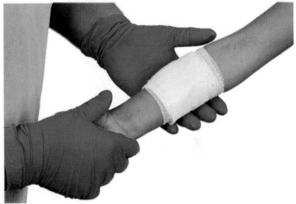

4 Tape or tie the end of the bandage in place.

Perform the Skill

Applying a Roller Bandage

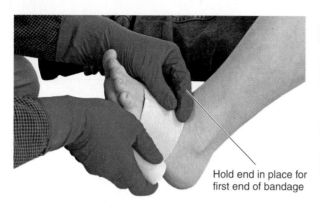

Hold end in place for
first end of bandage

1 Anchor the starting end of the bandage.

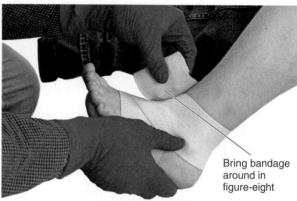

Bring bandage
around in
figure-eight

2 Turn bandage diagonally across top of foot and
around ankle.

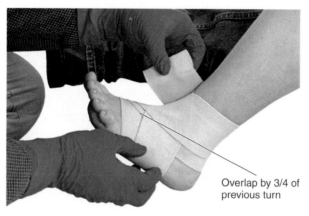

Overlap by 3/4 of
previous turn

3 Continue with overlapping figure-eight turns.

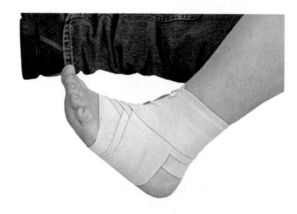

4 Fasten end of bandage with clips, tape, or safety
pins.

For simple closed wounds:

When You See

- Bruising
- Signs of pain

Do This First

1. Check for signs and symptoms of a fracture or sprain (see Chapter 7) and give appropriate first aid.
2. Put ice or a cold pack on the area to control bleeding, reduce swelling, and reduce pain.
3. With an arm or leg, wrap the area with an elastic bandage. Keep the part raised to help reduce swelling.

Additional Care

- Seek medical attention if you suspect a more serious injury such as a fracture or sprain
- Keep the child calm and distracted to ensure cooperation

For internal bleeding:

When You See

- Abdomen is tender, swollen, bruised, or hard
- Blood vomited or coughed up, or present in urine
- Cool, clammy skin, may be pale or bluish
- Thirst
- Possible confusion, light-headedness

Do This First

1. Lay the child down on the back with feet raised 8 to 12 inches.
2. Call 911.
3. Be alert for vomiting. Put a child who vomits or becomes unresponsive in the recovery position.
4. Maintain the child's body temperature.

Additional Care

- Calm and reassure the child
- If the child becomes unresponsive, monitor the ABCs and give basic life support (BLS) as needed
- Treat for shock (see Chapter 4)

Learning Checkpoint ④

1. True or False: To control bleeding, make a pressure bandage as tight as you can get it.

2. You have put a roller bandage around a child's arm to control bleeding from a laceration. A few minutes later she says her fingers are tingling. You feel her hand, and her fingers are cold. What should you do?

_____

3. When applying a bandage over a dressing, the bandage should:

   a. Hold down only the corners of the dressing so the wound can "breathe"

   b. Be soaked first in cold water

   c. Cover the entire dressing

   d. Be loose enough so it can be slid to one side to change the dressing

4. Name three ways you can secure the end of an elastic roller bandage.

_____

Chapter

4 Shock

CHAPTER PREVIEW

- Causes of Shock
- First Aid for Shock
- Anaphylaxis

Shock is a dangerous condition in which not enough oxygen-rich blood is reaching vital organs in the body. The brain, heart, and other organs need a continual supply of oxygen. Anything that happens to or in the body that significantly reduces blood flow can cause shock.

Shock is a life-threatening emergency. It may develop quickly or gradually. Always call 911 for a child in shock.

CAUSES OF SHOCK

- *Severe bleeding* causes shock when there is not enough blood circulating in the body to bring required oxygen to vital organs. This is the most common cause of shock in children. With internal injuries, it may not be obvious a child is bleeding inside.
- *Heart problems*, like a heart attack or heart rhythm problem, cause shock when the heart cannot pump enough blood to meet the body's needs.
- *Nervous system injuries*, such as those caused by neck or spine injuries, can affect the heart or blood vessels in ways that prevent adequate blood from reaching vital organs.

Many other types of injuries can also cause some degree of shock. Some specific examples are as follows:

- Dehydration (such as may occur in heatstroke or with severe vomiting or diarrhea)
- Serious infections
- Severe burns
- Allergic reactions (see later section on Anaphylaxis)
- Heart failure

FIRST AID FOR SHOCK

Shock has various signs and symptoms depending on its cause and severity. A child with any serious injury should be assumed to be at risk of shock, even if you do not see all these signs and symptoms (**Figure 4-1**).

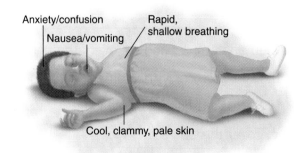

Anxiety/confusion

Nausea/vomiting

Rapid, shallow breathing

Cool, clammy, pale skin

Figure 4-1 Signs of shock.

When You See

- Anxiety, confusion, agitation, or restlessness
- Dizziness, light-headedness
- Cool, clammy or sweating, pale or bluish skin
- Rapid, shallow breathing
- Thirst
- Nausea, vomiting
- Changing levels of responsiveness

Do This First

1. Give basic life support (BLS) and care for life-threatening injuries.
2. Call 911.
3. Have the child lie on his or her back and raise the legs about 8 to 12 inches (unless the child may have a spine injury). Loosen any tight clothing (**Figure 4-2**).
4. Try to maintain the child's normal body temperature. If lying on the ground, put a coat or blanket under the child. If in doubt, keep the child warm with a blanket or coat over his or her body (**Figure 4-3**).

Additional Care

- Stay with the child and offer reassurance and comfort
- Put an unresponsive child (if spinal injury is not suspected) in the recovery position
- Keep bystanders from crowding around the child

ALERT

Shock

Do not let a child in shock eat or drink. Note that sweating in a child in shock is not necessarily a sign of being too warm. If in doubt, it is better to ensure the child's body temperature by keeping the child warm.

ANAPHYLAXIS

Anaphylaxis is a severe allergic reaction, also called anaphylactic shock. It is a life-threatening emergency because the child's airway may swell, making breathing difficult or impossible. Always call 911 for an anaphylaxis emergency. Common causes of anaphylaxis include:

- Certain drugs (such as penicillins, sulfa)
- Certain foods (such as peanuts, shellfish, eggs)
- Insect stings and bites (such as bees or wasps)

Some older children who know they have a severe allergy may carry an emergency epinephrine kit such as an EpiPen-Jr®. This medication can stop the anaphylactic reaction. Ask the child about this and help him or her open the kit. Follow your childcare center's policy to use the kit as needed. The EpiPen-Jr® is removed from its case and the cap removed. The tip is then jabbed into the muscle of the outer part of the thigh and held there five to ten seconds (**Figure 4-4**). The injection site is then massaged for a few seconds. The effects of the emergency

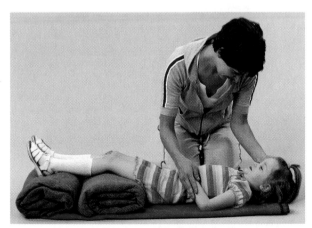

Figure 4-2 Raise the legs 8 to 12 inches.

Figure 4-3 Try to maintain the child's normal body temperature.

Learning
Checkpoint ①

1. True or False: Because a child in shock is thirsty and may be dehydrated, offer clear fluids to drink.

2. True or False: A spinal injury can cause shock.

3. Which of these actions should you take *first* for a child in shock because of external bleeding?

   a. Stop the bleeding

   b. Raise the legs

   c. Loosen constricting clothing

   d. Cover the child with a blanket

4. A child in shock is likely to have which signs and symptoms?

   a. Vomiting, diarrhea, red face

   b. Nausea, thirst, clammy skin

   c. Incontinence, hives, swollen legs

   d. Headache, painful abdomen, coughing

5. What is the most important action to take for *all* children in shock?

_____

epinephrine may last 10 to 20 minutes. A second dose may be needed and can be given 10 minutes after the first dose.

When You See
- Difficulty breathing, wheezing
- Complaints of tightness in throat or chest
- Swelling of the face and neck, puffy eyes
- Red, blotchy skin
- Anxiety, agitation
- Nausea, vomiting
- Changing levels of responsiveness

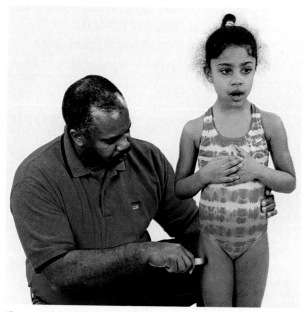

Figure 4-4 Using an EpiPen-Jr®.

Do This First

1. Call 911.

2. Give BLS as needed.

3. Help the child use his or her epinephrine kit.

4. Help the child sit up in position of easiest breathing (Figure 4-5).

Additional Care

- Stay with the child and offer reassurance and comfort
- Put an unresponsive child (if spinal injury is not suspected) in the recovery position

Figure 4-5 Help an anaphylactic child into the position of easiest breathing.

Learning
Checkpoint 2

1. True or False: Ask an older child having an anaphylactic reaction about any allergies.

2. True or False: A bee sting can cause a severe allergic reaction.

3. The major risk for a child in anaphylaxis is:

  a. Swelling around the eyes

  b. Heart attack

  c. Internal bleeding

  d. Breathing problems

4. How should a child in anaphylaxis be positioned if having trouble breathing?

_____

5 Burns

Burns of the skin or deeper tissues may be caused by heat, chemicals, or electricity. Mild heat burns and sunburn may need only simple first aid, but severe burns are a medical emergency. Burns are more common in children because many children have not learned safety guidelines around fire or heat sources.

HEAT BURNS

Heat burns may be caused by flames, contact with steam or any hot object, or sun exposure. The severity of a burn depends on the amount of damage to the skin and other tissues under the skin.

Put Out the Fire!

If a child's clothing is on fire, have him or her **stop, drop, and roll** (**Figure 5-1**). Use water to put out any flames. Even when the fire is out, the skin will keep burning if it is still hot, so cool the burn area with water immediately, except with very severe burns. Also remove the child's clothing and any jewelry, if possible without further injuring the child, because these items may still be hot and continue to burn the child.

How Bad Is the Burn?

- **First-degree burns** (also called superficial burns) damage only the skin's outer layer, like a sunburn. These are typically minor burns and usually heal by themselves.
- **Second-degree burns** (also called partial-thickness burns) damage the skin's deeper layers. When small they may not be too serious, but larger second-degree burns require medical attention.

- **Third-degree burns** (also called full-thickness burns) damage the skin all the way through and may burn the muscle or other tissues. These are medical emergencies (**Figure 5-2**).

Also important is the location of the burn on the body. Burns on the face, genitals, or hands or feet generally are more serious and require medical care.

First-Degree Burns (Including Sunburn)

When You See

- Skin is red, dry, and painful (**Figure 5-3**)
- May be some swelling
- Skin not broken

Do This First

1. Stop the burning by removing the heat source.
2. Cool the burned area with room temperature water. Immerse a small area in a sink or bucket, or cover a larger area (but not most of the body) with wet cloths for at least 10 minutes.
3. Remove clothing and jewelry or any other constricting item before the area swells.
4. Protect the burn from friction or pressure.

Additional Care

- Aloe vera gel can be used on the skin for comfort (follow your childcare center's policy)
- Give the child cool water to drink
- Follow your childcare center's policy on giving acetaminophen or ibuprofen for pain (parental permission required)

(b) Drop

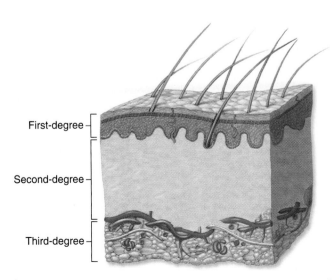

(a) Stop

(c) Roll

Figure 5-1 Teach children to stop, drop, and roll.

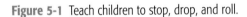

Figure 5-2 Depth of a burn.

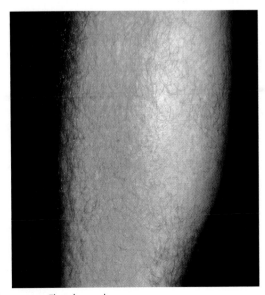

Figure 5-3 First-degree burn.

Burn

Do not put butter on a burn.
Do not use ice or cold water on a burn because
even though it may relieve pain, the cold can
actually cause additional damage to the skin.

Second-Degree Burns

When You See

- Skin is swollen and red, may be blotchy or streaked
- Blisters that may be weeping clear fluid (Figure 5-4)
- Signs of significant pain

Do This First

1. Stop the burning by removing the heat source.
2. Cool the burned area with room temperature water. Immerse a small area in a sink or bucket, or cover a larger area (but not most of the body) with wet cloths for at least 10 minutes or until the area is free of pain even after removal from the water.
3. Remove clothing and jewelry from the area before the area swells.
4. Put a dressing over the burn to protect the area, but keep it loose and do not tape it to the skin.

Additional Care

- For large burns or burns on the face, genitals, hands, or feet, seek medical attention. A young child with a second-degree burn more than an inch across needs medical attention.
- Follow your childcare center's policy to contact the child's parents

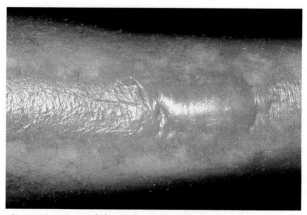

Figure 5-4 Second-degree burn.

Second-Degree Burn

Do not break skin blisters! This could cause an
infection. Be gentle when covering the area.
Do not remove any material sticking
to the burned area.

Third-Degree Burns

When You See

- Skin damage, charred skin, or white leathery skin (Figure 5-5)
- May have signs and symptoms of shock (pale, clammy skin; nausea and vomiting; fast breathing)

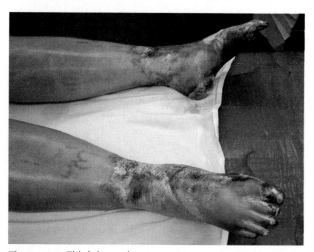

Figure 5-5 Third-degree burn.

Do This First

1. Stop the burning by removing the heat source.
2. Cool surrounding first- and second-degree burns only.
3. Remove clothing and jewelry before the area swells.
4. Call 911.
5. Prevent shock: have the child lie down, elevate the legs, and maintain normal body temperature.
6. Carefully cover the burn with a dressing. Do not apply a cream or ointment.

Additional Care

- Watch the child's breathing and be ready to give basic life support (BLS) if needed

Third-Degree Burn

With third-degree burns do not cool more than 10% of the child's body with water because of the risk of hypothermia and shock. Do not touch the burn or put anything on it. Do not remove any material sticking to the burned area. Do not give the child anything to drink.

Smoke Inhalation

Inhaling very hot air or smoke can burn the airway from the mouth to the lungs. This can be a medical emergency. Because the signs and symptoms from smoke inhalation may not become obvious for up to 48 hours after exposure, any child thought to have inhaled smoke should see a healthcare provider.

When You See

- Smoke visible in area
- Coughing, wheezing, hoarse voice
- Possible burned area on face or chest
- Difficulty breathing

Do This First

1. Get the child to fresh air, or fresh air to the child.
2. Call 911.
3. Help the child into a position for easy breathing.

Additional Care

- Put an unresponsive child in the recovery position
- Loosen any clothing around the neck
- Be ready to give BLS if needed

Learning Checkpoint ①

1. True or False: With a child with a second-degree burn, you should break skin blisters and then cover the area with a burn treatment ointment.

2. With a child with a third-degree burn, you should cool only a _____ area with water because of the risk of shock or hypothermia.

3. At a picnic a child gets too close to the barbecue and his clothing catches on fire. What do you do? List in correct order the first four actions you should take.

CHEMICAL BURNS

Many strong chemicals found in the home, childcare centers, and other settings can "burn" the skin on contact (**Figure 5-6**). See Chapters 15 and 16 for steps you can take to prevent children from contacting substances that can cause chemical burns. See Chapter 9 for chemicals on or in the mouth.

Sometimes the burn develops slowly, and in some cases the child may not even be aware of the burn at first. Both acids and alkalis, and liquids and solids can cause serious burns. Since the chemical reaction can continue as long as the substance is on the skin, you must flush it off with water as soon as possible.

When You See

- A chemical on the child's skin or clothing
- Complaints of pain or a burning sensation
- Skin redness or discoloration, blistering or peeling
- A spilled substance on or around an unresponsive child
- A smell of fumes in the air

Do This First

1. With a dry chemical, first brush it off the child's skin. (Wear medical exam gloves to prevent contact with the substance yourself.)
2. With a spilled liquid giving off fumes, move the child or ventilate the area.

3. Wash off the area as quickly as possible with running water for 30 to 60 minutes. Use a sink, hose, or even a shower to flush the whole area of contact.
4. Remove clothing and jewelry from the burn area.
5. Call 911 for large or deep chemical burns, or any burns on the child's face or head, hands or feet, or genital area.

Additional Care

- If chemicals were spilled in a confined area, leave the area with the child because of the risk of fumes.
- Put a dry dressing over the burn.
- A child with any chemical burn needs medical attention.

Chemicals in Eye

If a chemical splashes into a child's eye, flush the eye immediately with running water and continue for 20 minutes. If the child is wearing a contact lens, have him or her remove it. Tilt the child's head so that the water runs away from the face and not into the other eye. Call 911. After flushing, have the child hold a dressing over the eye until a healthcare provider is seen.

ELECTRICAL BURNS AND SHOCKS

Electrical burns may include:

- External burns caused by the heat of electricity
- Electrical injuries caused by electricity flowing through the body

External burns resulting from heat or flames caused by electricity are cared for the same as heat burns. Electrical injuries may cause only minor external burns where the electricity both entered and left the body (called entrance and exit wounds). But electricity flowing through the body can stop the heart and cause other serious injuries.

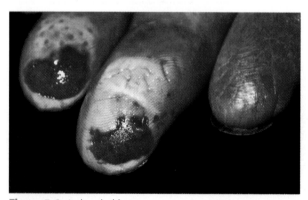

Figure 5-6 A chemical burn.

Learning
Checkpoint ②

1. A child has splashed a cleaning fluid in her eye and is crying and holding her hand over the eye. What should you do *first*?

   a. Have her keep holding the eye closed so that her tears will wash out the chemical

   b. Call 911 and wait for healthcare personnel to take care of her eye

   c. Immediately flush the eye with running water

   d. Mix baking soda with water and pour it into her eye

2. Describe the first action to take if a child has a dry chemical on the skin.

   _____

3. You enter a storage room that should have been locked and find an unresponsive child lying on the floor. Beside him is an open container and a puddle of a dark liquid. There's a strong smell in the air. What do you do?

   _____

ALERT

Electrical Shock

Do not touch a child you think has had an electrical shock! First make sure the power is turned off or the child is well away from the power source. Turn off the circuit breaker and call 911. Note that electrical burns can cause massive internal injuries even when the external burn may look minor.

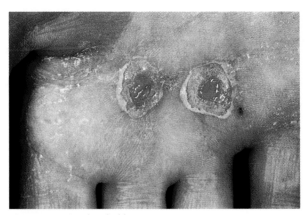

Figure 5-7 An electrical burn.

When You See

- A source of electricity near the child: bare wires, power cords, an electrical device
- Burned area of skin, possibly both entrance and exit wounds (Figure 5-7)
- Changing responsiveness

Do This First

1. Do not touch the child until you know the area is safe. Unplug or turn off the power.
2. With an unresponsive child, check the ABCs and give BLS as needed.
3. Call 911.
4. Care for the burn (stop the burning, cool the area, remove clothing and jewelry, cover the burn).
5. Prevent shock by having the child lie down, elevate the legs, and maintain normal body temperature.

Additional Care

- Keep an unresponsive child in the recovery position and monitor the ABCs until help arrives

LIGHTNING STRIKES

Lightning strikes often cause serious injury. In addition to burns, the electrical shock may affect the heart and brain and cause temporary blindness or deafness, unresponsiveness or seizures, bleeding, bone fractures, and cardiac arrest. Call 911 immediately and give BLS, treating the most serious injuries first.

Learning
Checkpoint ③

1. True or False: The first thing to do for an unresponsive child in contact with an electrical wire is pour water over the area of contact.

2. What is the safest way to stop the electricity when someone is shocked by an electrical appliance? How should you not try to stop it?

_____

3. A small child somehow crawled behind a desk in your childcare center, where you find her unresponsive with her hand on the computer power cord near the wall outlet. Your first action should be to:

a. Call 911

b. Grab her by the arms and pull her away from the power cord.

c. Turn the computer off

d. Pull out the power cord plug if you can do so safely, or turn off the circuit breaker

6 Serious Injuries

Many factors affect how serious a child's injury may be. As you have learned, injuries that threaten the child's airway, breathing, or circulation are life threatening. Severe bleeding is also very serious. This chapter describes some additional injuries in specific areas of the body that can be very serious for children and may become life threatening.

HEAD AND SPINAL INJURIES

Head injuries are common in children. Usually they are minor, such as a bump on the head (see Chapter 11), but with a more severe impact they may be serious. Any injury to a child's head may also injure the spine. Whenever you encounter a serious head injury, suspect a neck or spine injury also.

Skull Fractures

A skull fracture is life threatening. Call 911 immediately. Chapter 3 describes the signs and symptoms of a skull fracture and the first aid to give while waiting for help.

Brain Injuries

Brain injuries include bleeding, swelling, and concussion. A **concussion** is a temporary impairment of brain function and usually does not involve permanent damage. However, it is generally difficult to determine whether a child's injury is moderately or very serious, and the child may have a variety of signs and symptoms. Do not worry about trying to figure out what specifically is wrong with a head injury—just call 911 and give supportive care while waiting for help.

When You See

- Head wound suggesting there was a blow to the head
- Changing levels of responsiveness, drowsiness
- Difficulty being awakened
- Confusion, disorientation, memory loss about the injury
- Headache
- Dizziness
- Lack of coordination, clumsiness, abnormal speech
- Nausea, vomiting
- Unequal pupils (Figure 6-1)
- Convulsions

Do This First

For a responsive child:

1. Have the child lie down.
2. Keep the child still and help maintain the child's body temperature.
3. Call 911 and monitor the child's condition until help arrives.

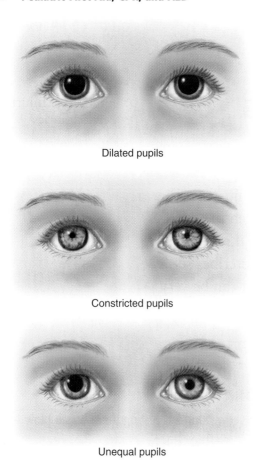

Dilated pupils

Constricted pupils

Unequal pupils

Figure 6-1 Check to see if a child's pupils are dilated, constricted, or uneven.

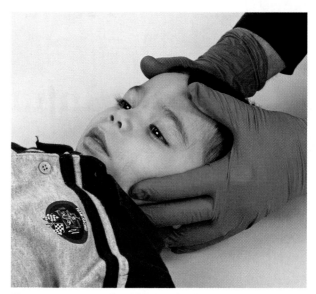

Figure 6-2 Support the child's head in line with his or her body for suspected spinal injury.

Brain Injury
Do not let the child eat or drink anything.
Do not give a pain medication.

For an unresponsive child:

1. Check the child's ABCs without moving the child unless necessary. Assume there may be a spinal injury.
2. Control serious bleeding and cover any wounds with a dressing.
3. Call 911.
4. If the child vomits, move him or her into the recovery position. If you suspect a spinal injury, support the child's head and neck at all times.

Additional Care

- Support the neck, even in a responsive child, if you suspect a spinal injury (**Figure 6-2**)

Later Signs and Symptoms

In some cases after a blow to the head the child does not have the signs and symptoms listed earlier and does not receive medical care. Signs and symptoms appearing within 48 hours may indicate a more serious injury, however, including nausea and vomiting, severe or persistent headache, altered or changing responsiveness, problems with vision or speech, or seizures. The child needs medical attention immediately if any of these occurs following a head injury.

Infants

Because an infant's skull bones are not completely formed and not yet as strong as an older child's, any infant who experiences a blow to the head should be seen by a healthcare provider. Call 911 immediately if the infant has any of the signs and symptoms described earlier for a child, and monitor the infant's ABCs.

Spinal Injuries

A fracture of the neck or back is a spinal injury. This injury may be life threatening and can cause permanent paralysis. It is very important not to move the child any more than necessary and to support the head and neck to prevent worsening of the injury. Do not let a child with a suspected spinal injury try to sit or stand up or move around, because any movement of the neck could damage nerves.

Suspect a spinal injury in these situations:

- A fall from a height (even a short height)
- A motor vehicle or bicycle crash
- A blow to the head or back
- A crushing injury of the head, neck, or back
- A diving injury

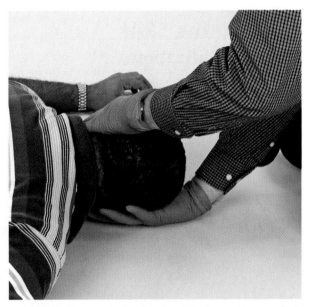

Figure 6-3 Support the head and neck in the position you find the child.

When You See

In a responsive child:
- Inability to move any body part
- Lack of sensation or tingling in hands or feet
- Deformed neck or back
- Breathing problems
- Headache

In an unresponsive child:
- Deformed neck or back
- Signs of blow to head or back
- Nature of the emergency suggests possible spinal injury

Do This First

1. Assess a responsive child:
   - Can the child move his or her fingers and toes?
   - Can the child feel you touch his or her hands and feet?
2. Stabilize the child's head and neck in the position found (**Figure 6-3**).

3. Monitor the child's ABCs. Use the jaw thrust to keep airway open if necessary in an unresponsive child.
4. Have someone call 911.
5. For a long wait, or if you must leave the child to call 911, use padding or heavy objects on both sides of head to prevent movement.

Additional Care

- Reassure a responsive child and tell him or her not to move
- Continue to monitor the child's ABCs until help arrives

Always support the child's head and neck in the position found. Move the child only if absolutely necessary, such as if a child lying on his or her back vomits. If this occurs, you must roll the child onto his or her side to let the mouth drain and allow breathing. The help of one or two others is necessary to keep the child's back and neck aligned during the move.

Perform the Skill
Inline Stabilization

See if the victim has feeling and can move hands and feet.

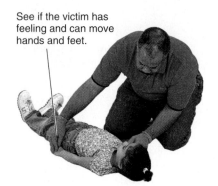

Do not pull on neck.

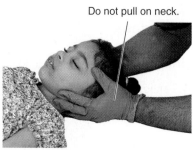

Use the jaw thrust to keep airway open if needed.

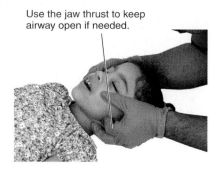

1 Assess a responsive child for spinal injury.

2 Hold the child's head with both hands to prevent movement of neck or spine.

3 Monitor the child's ABCs.

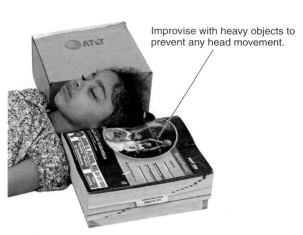

Improvise with heavy objects to prevent any head movement.

4 Have someone call 911.

5 Use objects to maintain head support if needed.

Perform the Skill

Rolling a Child with Spinal Injury (Log Roll)

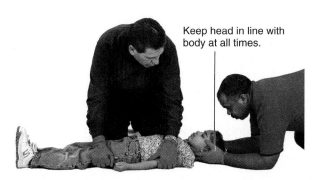

Keep head in line with body at all times.

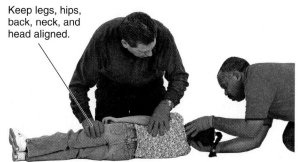

Keep legs, hips, back, neck, and head aligned.

1 Hold the child's head with your hands on both sides over ears.

2 The first aider at the child's head directs others to roll body as a unit.

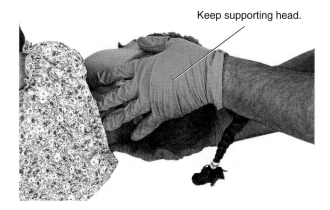

Keep supporting head.

3 Continue to support the child's head in the new position on his or her side.

Learning
Checkpoint 1

1. True or False: Suspect a spinal injury in any child with a serious head injury.

2. True or False: You can easily tell a mild concussion from a serious brain injury by the signs and symptoms.

3. Check off the possible signs and symptoms of a brain injury:

___ Headache   ___ Fingernail beds look blue

___ Rapid blinking   ___ Dizziness or confusion

___ Memory loss   ___ Nausea and vomiting

4. For an unresponsive child you suspect may have a spinal injury:

  a. First place the child on his or her back in case you have to give CPR

  b. Check the ABCs in the position in which you found the child

  c. Turn the head to one side in case the child vomits

  d. Move all body parts to see if anything feels broken

5. A spinal injury is likely in which of these situations? (Check all that apply.)

  ___ A child fell from a tree at a height of about 10 feet

  ___ A child on a skateboard ran into a telephone pole and is unresponsive

  ___ The child was in a car that hit a telephone pole

  ___ A piece of heavy equipment fell from a shelf on the child's head

6. Which of these are signs and symptoms of a spinal injury? (Check all that apply.)

  ___ Child cannot stop coughing   ___ Child's face is bright red

  ___ Child's hands are tingling   ___ Unresponsive child has nosebleed

  ___ Child has breathing problem   ___ Child's neck seems oddly turned

7. When do you call 911 for a child with a potential spinal injury?

  a. Call for all children with a potential spinal injury

  b. Call only if the child is unresponsive

  c. Call for a responsive child only if feeling is lost on one side of the child

  d. Call after waiting 10 minutes to see if an unresponsive child awakes

8. In what position do you stabilize the head of a child with a suspected spinal injury?

  _____

9. Roll a child with a spinal injury onto his or her side only if the child _____.

CHEST INJURIES

Serious chest injuries include broken ribs, objects impaled in the chest, and sucking chest wounds in which air passes in and out of the chest cavity. These wounds can be life threatening if breathing is affected. Chest injuries may result from such things as:

  • A motor vehicle crash
  • A blow to the chest
  • A fall from a height

The general signs and symptoms of a chest injury include:

  • Breathing problems
  • Severe pain
  • Deformity of the chest
  • Possibly coughing blood

Broken Ribs

When You See

- Signs of pain with deep breathing or movement
- Child holding ribs
- Shallow breathing

Do This First

1. Have child sit in position of easiest breathing.
2. Support the ribs with a pillow or soft padding (**Figure 6-4**). This can be loosely bandaged over the area and under the arm.
3. Call 911.

Additional Care

- Monitor the child's breathing while waiting for help, and provide BLS if needed
- If needed, immobilize the arm with a sling and binder (see Chapter 7) to prevent movement and ease pain

Figure 6-4 Support a rib fracture.

Impaled Object

Removing an impaled object from a child's chest could cause additional bleeding and breathing problems. If a child has an impaled object, leave it in place and seek medical attention.

When You See

- An object impaled in a chest wound

Do This First

1. Keep the child still. The child may be seated or lying down.
2. Use bulky dressings or cloth to stabilize the object.
3. Bandage the area around the object.
4. Call 911.

Additional Care

- Reassure the child
- Monitor the child's ABCs until help arrives

ALERT

Chest Injury
Do not give the child anything to eat or drink.

Sucking Chest Wound

A sucking chest wound is an open wound in the chest caused by a penetrating injury. The wound lets air move in and out of the chest during breathing. This wound can be life threatening because breathing can be affected.

When You See

- Air moving in or out of a penetrating chest wound

Do This First

1. Put a thin sterile dressing over the wound.
2. Cover the dressing with a plastic bag or wrap to make an air-tight seal. As the child exhales, tape it in place on three sides, leaving one side untaped to let exhaled air escape.
3. Position the child lying down inclined toward the injured side.
4. Call 911.

Additional Care

• If the child's breathing becomes more difficult, remove the plastic seal to let air escape; then reapply it
• Monitor the child's ABCs until help arrives

ABDOMINAL INJURIES

Abdominal injuries include closed and open wounds that result from a blow to the abdomen or a fall. These may involve internal and/or external bleeding, and organs may protrude from the wound. The child needs immediate medical care even if no significant injuries can be seen.

Closed Abdominal Injury

A closed abdominal injury can be life threatening because internal organs may have ruptured and there may be serious internal bleeding.

When You See

• Signs of severe pain, tenderness in area
• Bruising
• Swollen or rigid abdomen

Do This First

1. Carefully position the child on his or her back. Allow the child to bend the knees slightly if this eases the pain (support with a pillow under the knees).
2. Loosen any tight clothing.
3. Call 911.
4. Treat the child for shock and monitor the child's ABCs.

Additional Care

• Continue to monitor the child's ABCs until help arrives

Learning
Checkpoint ②

1. True or False: Broken ribs are treated by taping the entire ribcage tightly.

2. Immobilize the arm of a child with a rib fracture to

   a. Prevent movement   **c.** Help immobilize that side of the chest

   b. Ease pain   **d.** All of the above

3. What should you do with a piece of broken glass you see embedded in the chest of a child who has fallen off a bicycle?

_____

4. A child who fell on a sharp object on the ground has a small bleeding hole in the right side of his chest. You open his shirt to treat the bleeding and see air bubbles forming in the hole as air escapes. How do you dress this wound?

_____

Abdominal Injury
Do not let the child eat or drink.

Open Abdominal Wound

When You See

- Open abdominal wound
- Bleeding
- Organs possibly protruding from wound

Do This First

1. Lay the child on his or her back. Allow the child to bend the knees slightly if this eases the pain (support with a pillow under the knees).
2. Loosen any tight clothing.
3. If organs are protruding through the wound opening, do not try to push them back in.

Cover the wound with a dressing moistened with sterile or clean water, or plastic wrap if water is unavailable.

4. Cover the moistened dressing with a large dry sterile dressing and tape it loosely in place.
5. Call 911.
6. Treat the child for shock and monitor the child's ABCs.

Additional Care

- Continue to monitor the child's ABCs until help arrives

Open Abdominal Wound
Do not push protruding organs back inside the abdomen, but keep them from drying out with a moist dressing or plastic covering.

Learning Checkpoint ③

1. After an incident at a playground you find an unresponsive child on the ground, his shirt torn open. Which of the following are signs and symptoms he may have a closed abdominal injury? (Check all that apply.)

___ Bruises below the ribcage   ___ Pupils of eyes look small

___ Noisy breathing   ___ Swollen abdomen

___ Skin feels hot all over   ___ Skin around navel feels rigid

2. Describe the best position to put a child in with either an open or closed abdominal wound.

_____

_____

3. True or False: To treat a child for shock, help the child maintain normal body temperature.

4. If the child has an organ protruding from an open abdominal wound, what should you do?

   a. Push the organ back into the abdomen

   b. Put a clean, dry dressing over the wound

   c. Leave the wound exposed to the air

   d. Cover the wound with a moist dressing or plastic wrap

5. In what circumstances do you call 911 for a child with an open or closed abdominal wound?

PELVIC INJURIES

A broken pelvis may cause severe internal bleeding and organ damage. A broken pelvis can be a life-threatening injury.

When You See

- Signs of pain and tenderness around the hips
- Inability to walk or stand
- Signs and symptoms of shock

Do This First

1. Help the child lie on his or her back and bend knees slightly if this eases the pain (support with a pillow under the knees).
2. Immobilize the child's legs by placing padding between the thighs and ankles and then bandaging them together, unless this causes more pain (Figure 6-5).
3. Call 911.

4. Treat the child for shock and monitor the child's ABCs.

Additional Care

- Continue to monitor the child's ABCs until help arrives

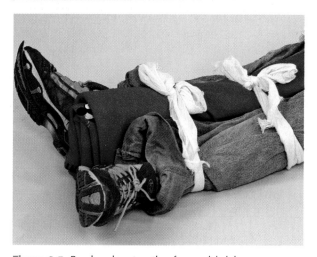

Figure 6-5 Bandage legs together for a pelvic injury.

Learning
Checkpoint ④

1. First aid for a pelvic fracture prevents _____ of the area.

2. True or False: Internal bleeding can be severe with a broken pelvis.

3. True or False: Bending the child's knees slightly may ease the pain of a broken pelvis.

7 Bone, Joint, and Muscle Injuries

Injuries of the bones, joints, and muscles are among the most common injuries in children. Fractures are generally the most serious, although dislocations and sprains can also be very serious. Fortunately, most musculoskeletal injuries do not involve fractures or dislocations.

FRACTURES

A **fracture** is a broken bone. The bone may be completely broken with the pieces separated, or it may be only cracked. With a **closed fracture** the skin is not broken. With an **open fracture** there is an open wound at the fracture site, and bone may protrude through the wound (**Figure 7-1**). Bleeding can be severe with fractures of large bones, and organs nearby may also be injured.

Closed   Open

Figure 7-1 Closed and open fractures.

When You See

- A deformed body part (compare to other side of body) (**Figure 7-2**)
- Signs of pain
- Swelling, discoloration of skin
- Inability to use the body part
- Bone exposed in a wound
- The child heard or felt a bone snap
- Possible signs and symptoms of shock

Do This First

1. Have the child rest and immobilize the area. With an extremity, also immobilize the joints above and below the fracture.
2. Call 911 for a large bone fracture. A child with a fractured hand or foot may be transported to the emergency room, following your childcare center's policy.
3. With an open fracture, cover the wound with a dressing and apply gentle pressure around the fracture area only if needed to control bleeding.

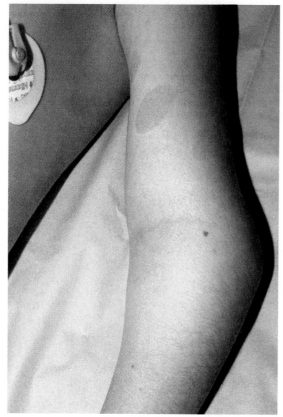

Figure 7-2 An obvious deformity may indicate a fracture.

JOINT INJURIES

Injuries to joints include dislocations and sprains. In a **dislocation,** one or more bones have been moved out of the normal position in a joint. A **sprain** is an injury to ligaments and other structures in a joint. Both kinds of joint injuries often look similar to a fracture.

Dislocations

It is not always possible to tell a dislocation from a closed fracture, but the first aid is very similar.

When You See

- The joint is deformed (compare to other side of body)
- Signs of pain
- Swelling
- Inability to use the body part

Do This First

1. Have the child rest. Immobilize the injured area in the position in which you find it (Figure 7-3).
2. Call 911. A child with a dislocated bone in the hand or foot may be transported to the emergency room, following your childcare center's policy.
3. Put ice or a cold pack on the area.
4. If help may be delayed or if the child is to be transported, use a splint to keep the area immobilized (see later section on splints).

Additional Care

- Treat the child for shock
- Monitor the child's ABCs
- Remove clothing and jewelry if they may cut off circulation as swelling occurs

4. Put ice or a cold pack on the area.
5. If help may be delayed or if the child is to be transported, use a splint to keep the area immobilized (see later section on splints). Elevate a splinted arm.

Additional Care

- Treat the child for shock as needed
- Monitor the child's ABCs
- Remove clothing and jewelry if they may cut off circulation as swelling occurs

Fracture
Do not try to align the ends of a broken bone. Do not give the child anything to eat or drink.

Dislocation
Do not try to put the displaced bone back in place. Do not let the child eat or drink.

Figure 7-3 Immobilize and support a dislocated shoulder.

Sprains

Sprains can range from mild to severe. It may be difficult to tell a severe sprain from a fracture, but the first aid is similar for both. The ankles, knees, wrists, and fingers are the body parts most often sprained.

When You See

- Signs of pain
- Swollen joint
- Bruising of joint area
- Inability to use joint

Do This First

1. Have the child rest. Immobilize the injured area in the position in which you find it.
2. Put ice or a cold pack on the area and then wrap joint with a compression bandage.
3. Use a soft splint (bandage, pillow, blanket) to immobilize and support the joint.
4. Elevate a sprained hand or ankle above the level of the heart (**Figure 7-4**).
5. Seek medical attention.

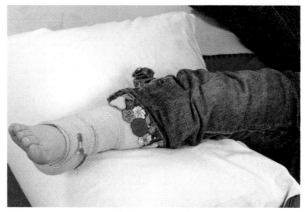

Figure 7-4 Support and elevate a sprain.

Additional Care

- Remove clothing or jewelry if they may cut off circulation as swelling occurs

MUSCLE INJURIES

Common muscle injuries include strains, contusions, and cramps. These injuries are usually less serious than bone and joint injuries.

Strains

A **strain** is a tearing of the muscle caused by overexerting or "pulling" a muscle. Strains are common sports injuries.

When You See

- Signs of dull or sharp pain when muscle is used
- Stiffness of the area
- Weakness or inability to use the muscle normally

Do This First

1. Rest the muscle.
2. Put ice or a cold pack on the area: 30 minutes on, then at least 30 minutes off.
3. With an extremity, wrap a compression bandage around the muscle.
4. Elevate the limb.

Learning
Checkpoint ①

1. True or False: Call 911 for a fracture of a large bone such as the thigh bone.

2. When immobilizing a fracture injury, what body area should be immobilized?

   a. The immediate fracture area

   b. The fracture area and the joint above it

   c. The fracture area and the joints both above and below it

   d. The entire child

3. True or False: With a fracture, you may also need to treat the child for shock.

4. The signs and symptoms of a bone or joint injury include which of the following? (Check all that apply.)

   ___ Deformed area   ___ Pain

   ___ Small or unequal pupils   ___ Inability to use part

   ___ Skin is hot and red   ___ Fever

   ___ Swelling   ___ Spasms and jerking of nearby muscles

5. True or False: A child with a sprained ankle should "walk it off."

Additional Care

- Seek medical attention if pain is severe or persists

Contusions

A **contusion** is a bruised muscle as may result from a blow.

When You See

- Signs of pain
- Swollen, tender area
- Skin discoloration (black and blue)

Do This First

1. Rest the muscle.

2. Put ice or a cold pack on the area: 30 minutes on, then at least 30 minutes off for the first 2 to 3 hours.

3. With an extremity, wrap a compression bandage around the muscle.

4. Elevate the limb.

Additional Care

- Seek medical attention if pain is severe or persists

Cramps

A muscle cramp is a tightening of a muscle usually caused by prolonged use. Cramps are common in the legs, stomach, back, or any muscle that is overused. These cramps are different from heat cramps, which result from fluid loss in hot environments (see Chapter 10).

When You See

• Signs of muscle pain and tightness

Do This First

1. Gently stretch out the muscle if possible.
2. Massage the muscle.

Additional Care

• Have the child drink plenty of fluids

RICE

The RICE acronym is an easy way to remember how to treat all bone, joint, and muscle injuries. With this procedure you do not have to know whether the injury is a fracture, dislocation, sprain, or strain, because they are treated in the same manner.

R = Rest
I = Ice
C = Compression
E = Elevation

Rest

Any movement of a musculoskeletal injury can cause further injury, pain, and swelling. Have the child rest until medical help arrives. Rest is also important for healing.

Ice

Cold reduces swelling, lessens pain, and minimizes bruising. Put ice or a cold pack on the injury (except for an open fracture) as soon as possible. Cubed or crushed ice in a plastic bag, or an improvised cold pack such as a bag of frozen peas or a cloth pad soaked in cold water (refreshed with cold water every 10 minutes), can be applied directly on the injured area. A commercial cold pack should be wrapped in cloth to prevent direct skin contact because it may be cold enough to freeze the skin.

Cold works best if applied to the injury as soon as possible, preferably within 10 minutes. Apply it for 30 minutes on and 30 minutes off for the first few hours, then for 20 to 30 minutes at a time every 2 or 3 hours for the first 24 to 48 hours, or for 72 hours for severe injuries.

Compression

Compression of an injured extremity is done with an elastic roller bandage. Compression helps prevent internal bleeding and swelling. Wrap the bandage over the injured area. It can also be used around a cold pack. Check the child's fingers or toes frequently to make sure circulation is not cut off.

Elevation

Elevating an injured arm or leg also helps prevent swelling and control internal or external bleeding. Splint a fracture first, and elevate it only if moving the limb does not cause pain.

SPLINTING THE EXTREMITIES

In most childcare centers, splinting is seldom used because medical help will arrive soon and because moving the injured area to apply the

Learning
Checkpoint ②

1. True or False: For a muscle strain, keep an ice pack on the injury for at least two hours.

2. True or False: Vigorous massage is the best treatment for a muscle contusion.

3. True or False: You can tell a contusion from a fracture because only a contusion causes an area of skin discoloration.

4. Name two things you can do to ease a muscle cramp.

Perform the Skill

RICE

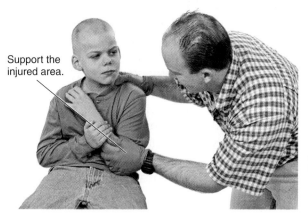

Support the injured area.

1 Rest the injured area.

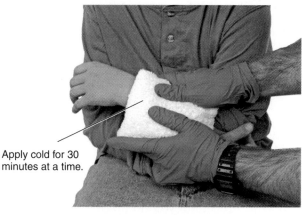

Apply cold for 30 minutes at a time.

2 Put ice or cold pack on the injured area.

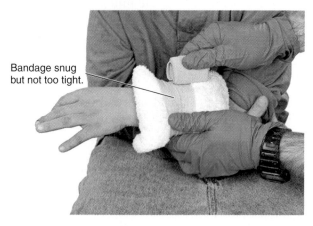

Bandage snug but not too tight.

3 Compress the injured area with an elastic roller bandage.

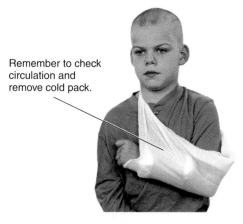

Remember to check circulation and remove cold pack.

4 Elevate the injured area using a sling.

splint may cause additional damage. In these cases it is generally recommended to help prevent movement of the injured area with pillows or other thick, soft padding.

In some other situations, however, when a child has a fracture, dislocation, or sprain in an arm or leg, the arm or leg may be splinted if the child is at risk for moving the injured area—unless help is expected within a few minutes. Always splint an extremity before transporting a child to a healthcare provider or emergency room. Splinting helps prevent further injury, reduces pain, and minimizes bleeding and swelling.

Types of Splints and Slings

Splints can be made from many different materials at hand (**Figure 7-5**). There are three types of splints:

- **Rigid splints** may be made from a board, a piece of plastic or metal, a rolled newspaper or magazine, or thick cardboard

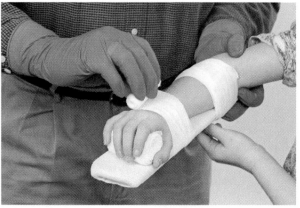

(a) Rigid splint.

(b) Soft splint.

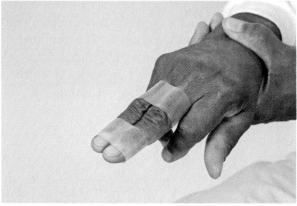

(c) Anatomic splint.

Figure 7-5 Examples of splints.

- **Soft splints** may be made from a pillow, folded blanket or towel, or a triangular bandage folded into a sling
- **Anatomic splints** involve splinting an injured leg to the uninjured leg or splinting fingers together

Splints can be tied in place with bandages, belts, neckties, or strips of cloth torn from clothing.

Guidelines for Splinting

- Put a dressing on any open wound before splinting the area
- Splint only if it does not cause more pain for the child
- Splint the injury in the position you find it (**Figure 7-6**)
- Splint to immobilize the entire area. With an extremity, splint the joints above and below the injured area.
- Put padding such as cloth between the splint and the skin
- Put splints on both sides of a fractured bone if possible
- Elevate the splinted extremity if possible
- Apply ice or a cold pack to the injury around the splint
- With a splinted extremity, check the child's fingers or toes frequently to make sure circulation is not cut off. Swelling, bluish discoloration, tingling or numbness, and cold skin are signs and symptoms of reduced circulation. If any of these are noted, the splint should be removed

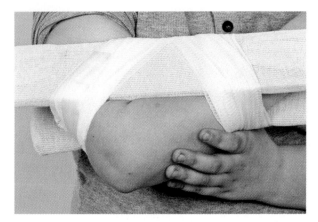 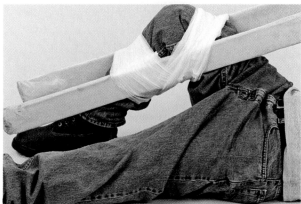

Figure 7-6 Splint an injury in the position found, such as these elbow and knee injuries. Do not try to straighten the limb to splint it.

Follow the steps shown in the following skill examples to splint an arm or leg. After splinting an arm, secure with a sling and binder. A sling supports and elevates an injury of the hand or forearm. A sling may also be used to minimize movement and support the area with a shoulder dislocation or rib fracture. A leg fracture can be splinted using either a rigid splint or an anatomic splint (as shown in the example). The example shows splinting of a lower leg fracture. A similar splint can be used for an upper leg fracture, with the bandages tied higher (including the hips).

Perform the Skill

Splinting an Arm

Support above and below the injury.

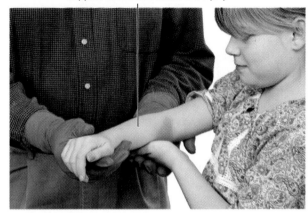

1 Support the arm.

If available, add a roller bandage.   Pad the splint.

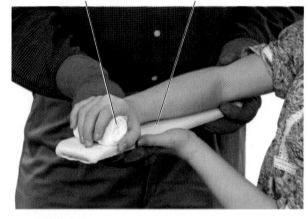

2 Position the arm on a rigid splint.

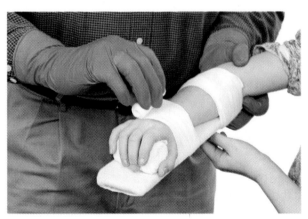

3 Secure the splint.

Check for tingling or numbness, swelling or cold skin.

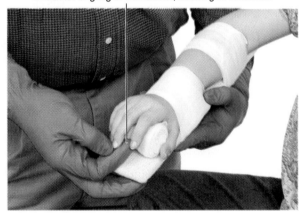

4 Check circulation.

Perform the Skill

Making an Arm Sling and Binder

Victim supports arm.

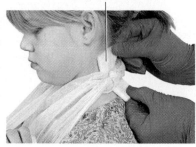

Pad under the knot.

1 Position the triangular bandage.

2 Bring up the lower end of the bandage to the opposite side of the neck.

3 Tie the ends.

Use a safety pin or tie the point at the elbow.

A binder helps prevent movement.

4 Secure the point of the bandage at the elbow.

5 Tie a binder bandage over the sling and around the chest.

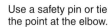

Perform the Skill

Splinting a Leg

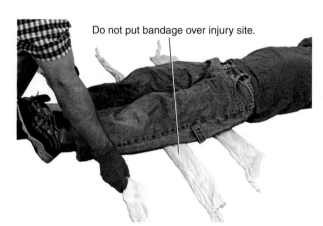

Do not put bandage over injury site.

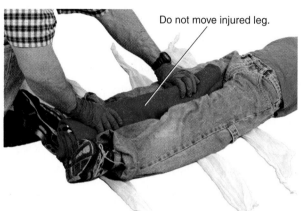

Do not move injured leg.

1 Gently slide 2 or 3 bandages or strips of cloth under both legs.

2 Put padding between the legs.

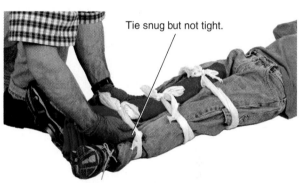

Tie snug but not tight.

3 Gently slide the uninjured leg next to the injured leg.

4 Tie the bandages.

Learning
Checkpoint ③

1. Use RICE for:

    a. Most musculoskeletal injuries

    b. Fractures only

    c. Muscle injuries only

    d. Muscle and joint injuries only

2. True or False: Putting a commercial cold pack directly on the skin is the best way to relieve pain and reduce swelling.

3. What is important about how you apply a compression bandage?

    a. Use elastic roller bandage

    b. Put the cold pack under the bandage

    c. Check that circulation is not cut off

    d. All of the above

4. Describe the steps you would follow to use RICE for a fractured or sprained ankle.

_____

5. A child falls in the yard outside your childcare center and has an obviously fractured forearm. What materials might you be able to find that you can use to make a rigid splint?

_____

6. When using a splint, which of the following actions should you take? (Check all that apply.)

____ Put a heating pad on the area   ____ Pad the splint

____ Straighten out a limb before splinting it   ____ Put a cold pack around splint

____ Dress an open wound before splinting   ____ Splint in position found

7. You find a child lying on the ground in the playground with obvious severe pain in one leg. You cannot tell whether the bone is broken, but there is no open wound and the child says it really hurts to move the leg. What should you do?

_____

Chapter

8 Sudden Illness

CHAPTER PREVIEW

- Meningitis
- Dehydration
- Near Drowning
- Asthma
- Croup
- Hyperventilation
- Respiratory Distress
- Fainting
- Seizures
- Severe Abdominal Pain
- Diabetic Emergencies

The illnesses described in this chapter may occur in children suddenly or without much warning that the child is becoming ill. In many cases the child's condition can rapidly become serious or life threatening, and you need to act quickly. In a childcare center, follow the center's policy for when to take action in an emergency and when to call the child's parents for less urgent medical care.

The following sections describe sudden illnesses that may affect children. You do not have to know for sure what the child's specific illness is, however, before you give first aid.

General signs and symptoms of sudden illness:

- Child feels ill, dizzy, confused, or weak
- Skin color changes (flushed or pale), sweating
- Nausea, vomiting

General care for sudden illness:

1. Call 911 for unexplained sudden illness.
2. Help the child rest and avoid getting chilled or overheated.
3. Reassure the child.
4. Do not give the child anything to eat or drink.
5. Watch for changes, and be prepared to give basic life support (BLS).

MENINGITIS

Meningitis is an inflammation of the meninges, the covering of the brain and spinal cord. It is a rare but life-threatening emergency. This disease is contagious and usually occurs in outbreaks. The signs and symptoms often come on quickly.

When You See

- Fever
- Chills
- Nausea, vomiting, loss of appetite

- Stiff neck
- Headache
- Convulsions
- Sensitivity to light

Do This First

1. If you suspect meningitis, or the child has been exposed to meningitis, call 911 or a healthcare provider immediately.
2. Keep the child comfortable and resting until seen by a healthcare provider.

Additional Care

- Keep other children away from a child suspected of having meningitis

DEHYDRATION

Dehydration occurs when the child loses significant amounts of body fluids, as may occur with heat exhaustion (see Chapter 10), diarrhea, or vomiting. Dehydration in infants and young children can be a serious condition.

When You See

- Sunken eyes
- Listlessness
- Dry mouth
- Infrequent urination and concentrated urine

Do This First

1. Give frequent drinks of clear fluids.
2. Seek medical attention if the infant or child will not drink or has repeated vomiting or diarrhea.

NEAR DROWNING

Infants and small children can drown quickly in a bath or pool. **Near drowning** is a condition that occurs when the child has been under water a prolonged time but may still be resuscitated. Note that children immersed in cold water have been successfully resuscitated after a lengthy time.

When You See

- An unresponsive child in water

Do This First

1. Remove the child from water, carrying the child with head lower than chest.
2. Have someone call 911 immediately. Check the ABCs. If you are alone and the child needs rescue breathing or CPR (see Chapter 2), give help for one minute before calling 911 yourself. Then continue BLS.
3. Be prepared for vomiting and to turn the child on his or her side.
4. If the child has signs of circulation and is breathing, place him or her in the recovery position.

Additional Care

- Call 911 even if the child recovers, because water in the lungs may still cause damage

ASTHMA

Asthma is a common problem affecting one in seven children. In an asthma attack the airway becomes narrow and the child has difficulty breathing. Most children with asthma you will encounter in a childcare setting have already been diagnosed and will have prescribed medication for emergency situations. You should be prepared to help the child with this medication following your childcare center's policy (**Figure 8-1**). Untreated, a severe asthma attack can be fatal.

Asthma Triggers

Asthma attacks are usually triggered by some factor in the child's internal or external environment. Understanding these factors helps prevent or minimize a child's attacks. Common triggers include:

- Respiratory infection, including the common cold (most common cause in children under age five)
- Allergic reaction to pollen, mold, dust mites, animal fur or dander

Figure 8-1 Many children with asthma use an inhaler with a spacer.

- Exercise (especially in cold, dry air)
- Certain foods (nuts, eggs, milk)
- Emotional stress
- Medications
- Air pollution caused by such things as cigarette smoke, vehicle exhaust, or fumes of cleaning products
- Temperature extremes

Knowing the specific triggers that provoke a child's asthma can help you prevent attacks. The child may have had a skin test to detect specific allergens that trigger his or her asthma. In addition to keeping the child away from the factors listed above, follow these guidelines:

- Use a damp cloth to dust furniture and surfaces
- Vacuum rugs frequently (when the child is not present)
- Avoid fluffy blankets and pillows that collect dust and those that contain feathers
- Enclose mattress and pillow in plastic covers
- Do not use air fresheners or products with strong odors
- Use an air purifier and keep child indoors when pollen counts are high

The Child's Treatment Plan

When a child has been diagnosed with asthma, the healthcare provider should provide a detailed management plan. A childcare center should have a copy of this plan. It should include:

- Activities and triggers to avoid
- How to treat the child's asthma
- Prescribed medications and when and how to use them
- What to do and who to call in an emergency

Know where this plan and the child's medications are kept and what to do if an asthma or other breathing emergency occurs. Note that in some states, childcare providers are required to have specific information on the use of inhaled medications.

When You See
- Wheezing and difficulty breathing and speaking
- Dry, persistent cough
- Fear, anxiety, fatigue, restlessness
- Gray-blue skin
- Changing levels responsiveness

Do This First
1. If the child is not known to have asthma (first attack), call 911 immediately.
2. If the child is known to have asthma, help the child use his or her medication (usually an inhaler).
3. Help the child rest and sit in a position for easiest breathing.
4. The child may use the inhaler again in 5 to 10 minutes if needed (follow specific instructions for this child).

Additional Care
- If the breathing difficulty persists after using the inhaler, call 911

Using a Peak Flow Meter

A **peak flow meter** is a device used to monitor the child's breathing ability—it is not used when an asthma attack occurs. The child's treatment plan may call for use of the peak flow meter at routine times and recording or charting the results. The meter is used this way:

1. The child takes a full breath in.
2. The child seals his or her lips around the mouthpiece and exhales out as hard and fast as possible.
3. The reading is taken from the position of the pointer on the meter.

How to Use a Metered-Dose Inhaler

Always follow the healthcare provider's specific instructions for helping a child use his or her inhaler, a device that contains and delivers the asthma medication. Following are general instructions that may need to be modified for the specific medication device or a particular child.

1. Shake the inhaler.
2. If a spacer is used, position it on the inhaler. (A spacer is a tube or chamber that fits between the inhaler and the child's mouth.)
3. Have the child breathe out fully through the mouth.
4. With the child's lips around the inhaler mouthpiece or the spacer, have the child inhale slowly and deeply; press the inhaler down to release one spray of medication as the child inhales. (A facemask is generally used for an infant instead of a mouthpiece.)
5. Have the child hold his or her breath for up to 10 seconds if possible and then exhale slowly. Follow the directions for the inhaler or the child's treatment plan to repeat doses if needed.

Asthma Inhaler

Use only the child's own prescribed inhaler—never use a child's inhaler with a different child.

How to Use a Nebulizer

Some children use a nebulizer rather than an inhaler to administer their asthma medication. A **nebulizer** uses an air compressor to make a fine mist of the medication for the child to breathe. Nebulizer equipment includes a compressor with tubing to a nebulizer cup attached to a mouthpiece or face mask (**Figure 8-2**). As with an inhaler, follow the specific instructions from the equipment manufacturer and healthcare provider. Following are the general instructions that may need to be modified for the specific device or a particular child.

1. Have the child sit in a quiet place away from other children.
2. Assemble the equipment.
3. Measure the medication and place it in the nebulizer cup.
4. Plug in the compressor and turn it on.
5. Using either the mouthpiece or mask, have the child breathe slowly and deeply until the medication cup is empty (**Figure 8-3**).

The nebulizer equipment should be cleaned after each use, following the equipment manufacturer's instructions. Generally, you take the pieces apart, wash the plastic pieces with soap and water, and let them dry. Note that lemon-scented or other strongly perfumed soap should not be used to wash this equipment because a perfumed soap can be irritating to someone with lung disease. The compressor may be wiped clean. The air filter on the compressor is periodically replaced. Store the unit in its container.

CROUP

Croup is an inflammation of the airway caused by a viral infection and is common in children between three months and six years of age. The symptoms are usually mild, but severe breathing difficulty requires medical attention.

When You See

- Barking cough
- Harsh noisy breathing (especially when inhaling)

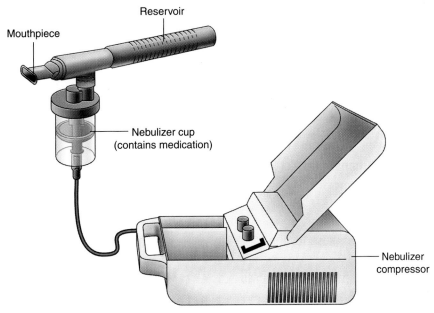

Figure 8-2 Parts of a nebulizer.

Figure 8-3 Child using a nebulizer.

Do This First

1. For severe breathing difficulty, seek immediate medical attention.
2. Help child sit up comfortably, or hold a small child, in position for easiest breathing.
3. Use a cool mist or steam vaporizer, and have the child breathe in the moist air. (If a vaporizer is not available, steam up the bathroom by running a hot shower.)

Additional Care

- If the attack of croup lasts longer than 15 minutes or seems severe, seek medical attention
- If the child has not recovered from the viral infection within a few days, a healthcare provider should be seen

- Use of head, neck, and abdominal muscles in breathing
- With breathing difficulty: bluish color of tongue and lips

Steam Vaporizer

If the vaporizer produces hot steam, do not let child get too close to it.

HYPERVENTILATION

Hyperventilation is fast, deep breathing caused by anxiety or stress.

When You See

- Very fast breathing rate
- Dizziness, faintness
- Tingling or numbness in hands and feet
- Muscle twitching or cramping

Do This First

1. Make sure there is no other cause for the breathing difficulty to care for.
2. Reassure the child and ask him or her to try to breathe slowly.
3. Call 911 if the child's breathing does not return to normal within a few minutes.

Additional Care

- A child who often has this problem should see a healthcare provider, because some medical conditions can cause rapid breathing

RESPIRATORY DISTRESS

Respiratory distress, or difficulty breathing, can be caused by many different illnesses and injuries. If you can know the cause of a child's breathing difficulty, such as asthma or croup (described earlier), give first aid for that problem. Otherwise, give the general breathing care described below.

When You See

- Child is gasping or unable to catch his or her breath
- Breathing is faster or slower, or deeper or shallower, than normal
- Breathing involves sounds such as wheezing or gurgling
- Child feels dizzy or lightheaded

Do This First

1. Call 911 for sudden unexplained breathing problems.
2. Help the child rest in position of easiest breathing.
3. If you have a prescribed medicine for the child, follow your childcare center's policy to help the child take it if needed.
4. Stay with the child and be prepared to give BLS.

Additional Care

- Calm and reassure the child (anxiety increases breathing distress)

Learning Checkpoint ①

1. True or False: Do not give a child with sudden illness anything to eat or drink.

2. If you suspect a child has meningitis, what is the first thing you should do?
   a. Position the child for easiest breathing
   b. Put the child in a darkened room
   c. Give medication for fever and headache, following your childcare center's policy
   d. Call 911

3. When do you seek medical attention for a child with dehydration?

4. If you are alone with a near-drowning child, what should you do?

    a. Leave the child and call 911

    b. Check the child's ABCs and give one minute of care before calling 911

    c. Rush the child to an emergency room

    d. Pump the child's abdomen to get water out of his or her body

5. What is the best thing a child with asthma can do when having an asthma attack?

_____

6. True or False: You cannot give first aid for a person with difficulty breathing unless you know the specific cause of the problem.

7. To help a child breathe easier:

    a. Position the child flat on his or her back

    b. Have the child stand, and clap him or her on the back with each breath

    c. Have the child sit and put his or her head between the knees

    d. Let the child find the position in which he or she can breathe most easily

8. The first aid for a child with croup includes:

    a. Use of a cool mist vaporizer

    b. Positioning the child on his or her back and raising the legs

    c. Immediately calling 911

    d. Using the child's inhaler

9. When should you call 911 for a child who seems to be hyperventilating?

_____

FAINTING

Fainting is caused by a temporary reduced blood flow to the brain. This commonly occurs in hot weather or after a prolonged period of inactivity, or from other causes such as pain, fright, or lack of food. If a child seems about to faint (feeling weak and dizzy, with a very pale face), have the child sit with head between the knees, or lie down with legs raised 8 to 12 inches (**Figure 8-4**).

When You See

- Sudden brief loss of responsiveness and collapse
- Pale, cool skin, sweating

Do This First

1. Check the child's ABCs and provide BLS if needed.
2. Lay the child down and raise the legs 8 to 12 inches. Loosen any tight clothing.

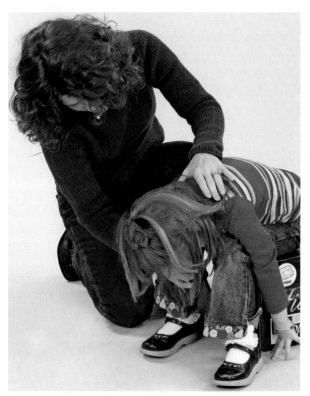

Figure 8-4 Position for a child about to faint.

3. Check for possible injuries caused by falling.

4. Reassure the child as he or she recovers.

Additional Care

- Call 911 if the child does not regain responsiveness soon or faints repeatedly
- Place an unresponsive child who is breathing in the recovery position to let the mouth drain in case of vomiting

ALERT

Fainting
Do not give a child who feels faint anything to drink.

Seizures

Seizures, or convulsions, result from a brain disturbance caused by many different conditions, including epilepsy, high fever in young children, certain injuries, and electric shock.

When You See

- *Minor seizures:* staring blankly ahead; slight twitching of lips, head, or arms and legs; other movements such as lip-smacking or chewing
- *Major seizures:* crying out and then becoming unresponsive; body becomes rigid and then shakes in convulsions; jaw may clench
- *Fever convulsions in young children:* hot, flushed skin; violent muscle twitching; arched back; clenched fists

Do This First

1. Try to catch a child who is about to fall. Prevent injury during the seizure by moving away dangerous objects and putting something flat and soft (or your hand) under the child's head (Figure 8-5).

2. Loosen clothing around the neck to ease breathing.

3. Gently turn the child onto one side to help keep the airway clear if vomiting occurs.

4. Monitor the ABCs and give BLS if needed.

5. Be reassuring as the child regains responsiveness.

Additional Care

- Call 911 if the seizure lasts more than five minutes, if the child is not known to have epilepsy, if the child does not recover within ten minutes, if the child has trouble breathing or has another seizure, if the child is known to have another medical condition, or if the child is injured
- For an infant or child with fever convulsions, sponge the body with room temperature water to help cool the body, and call 911

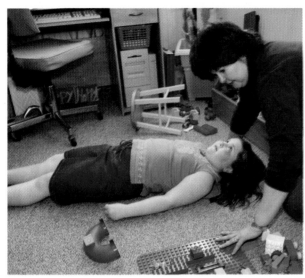

Figure 8-5 Protect a child from injury during a seizure.

ALERT

Seizure
Do not try to stop the child's movements.
Do not place any objects in the child's mouth.

Fever Convulsions

Younger children (generally between six months and four years of age) may have a seizure because of a rapidly rising fever. These are sometimes called **febrile seizures.** Give the same care for the seizure as described earlier, and then try to cool the child's body. Remove clothing and sponge the child's body with room temperature water; do not let the child get cold. Seek urgent medical attention.

SEVERE ABDOMINAL PAIN

Abdominal injuries are described in Chapter 6; always call 911 for an abdominal injury. Abdominal pain may also result from illness ranging from minor conditions to serious medical emergencies. Urgent medical care is needed for any severe abdominal pain in these situations:

- Sudden, severe, intolerable pain, or pain that causes awakening from sleep

- Pain that begins in the general area of the central abdomen and later moves to the lower right
- Pain with a swollen abdomen that feels hard
- Pain with a hard lump in lower abdomen or groin area
- Pain accompanied by difficulty breathing
- Pain that occurs suddenly, stops, and then returns without warning
- Pain accompanied by red or purple, jelly-like stool; or with blood or mucus in stool
- Pain accompanied by greenish-brown vomit

Appendicitis

Appendicitis, or inflammation of the appendix, may occur in a child of any age. Waves of pain begin in the middle of the abdomen and settle in severe pain in the right lower abdomen, along with fever, nausea with or without vomiting or diarrhea, and loss of appetite (**Figure 8-6**). Have the child lie down, and call 911 immediately. Do not give the child anything to eat or drink.

DIABETIC EMERGENCIES

Children with diabetes generally require daily insulin injections. Their meals and activity levels must also be regulated to maintain a balance of blood sugar and insulin in the body. Childcare providers should be aware of a child's diabetes and have received instructions from the parents on managing this condition and problems that

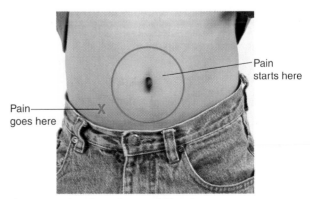

Figure 8-6 Locations of appendicitis pain.

may occur. Low blood sugar is called **hypogly-cemia,** and high blood sugar is called **hypergly-cemia.** Many factors can cause either of these conditions, which are more common in children with undiagnosed or newly diagnosed diabetes. Hypoglycemia is more common and often occurs quickly. Either condition can quickly progress to a medical emergency if the child is not treated.

Low Blood Sugar

When You See

- Sudden dizziness, weakness, shakiness, or mood change (irritability or combativeness)
- Headache, confusion, difficulty paying attention
- Pale skin, sweating
- Hunger
- Clumsy, jerky movements
- Possible seizure

Do This First

1. Confirm that the child is known to have diabetes; look for a medical ID. Follow your childcare center's instructions for how much sugar to give the child.
2. Give a fully responsive child sugar: glucose tablets, fruit juice, sugar packets (but *not* non-sugar sweetener packets), or hard candy (unless choking is a risk) **(Figure 8-7)**.
3. Call 911 immediately so that EMS personnel can assess the child and provide additional treatment as needed.
4. If after 15 minutes EMS has not responded and the child still feels ill or has signs and symptoms, give more sugar.

Additional Care

- If the child becomes unresponsive or continues to have significant signs and symptoms, monitor the ABCs and provide BLS while waiting for help

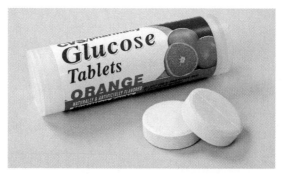

Figure 8-7 Glucose tablets.

Diabetic Emergency Alert!
If a diabetic child becomes unresponsive, do not try to inject insulin or put food or fluids in the mouth.

High Blood Sugar

When You See

- Frequent urination
- Drowsiness
- Dry mouth, thirst
- Shortness of breath, deep rapid breathing
- Breath smells fruity
- Nausea, vomiting
- Eventual unresponsiveness

Do This First

1. Confirm that the child has diabetes; look for a medical ID.
2. Follow the child's healthcare provider's instructions for hyperglycemia.
3. If you cannot judge whether the child has low or high blood sugar, give sugar as for low blood sugar. Call 911.
4. Call 911 if the child becomes unresponsive or continues to have significant signs and symptoms.

Additional Care

- Put an unresponsive child who is breathing in the recovery position and monitor the ABCs

Learning
Checkpoint ②

1. When should you call 911 for a child who faints?

_____

2. True or False: When a child faints, lay him or her down and raise the head and shoulders 8 to 12 inches.

3. For a child having seizures:

   a. Lay the child face down on the floor

   b. Ask others to help you hold the child's head, arms, and legs still

   c. Put something flat and soft under the child's head

   d. Put something wood, like a pencil, between the child's teeth

4. Name at least three situations in which you should call 911 for a child who has a seizure.

_____

5. What should you do for a young child whose abdomen is swollen and feels hard?

_____

6. Check off common signs and symptoms of a low blood sugar diabetic emergency:

   ___ **a.** Dizziness   ___ **e.** Red, blotchy skin

   ___ **b.** Hunger   ___ **f.** Sweating

   ___ **c.** Rapid deep breathing   ___ **g.** Confusion

   ___ **d.** Clumsiness   ___ **h.** Swollen legs

9 Poisoning

Poisoning is a common emergency in young children.

SWALLOWED POISONS

Many substances in home and childcare settings are poisonous if swallowed.

When You See

- Open container of poisonous substance
- A burn or smell around the child's mouth
- Nausea, vomiting, abdominal cramps
- Drowsiness, dizziness, disorientation
- Changing levels of responsiveness

Do This First

1. Clean any remaining poison from the child's mouth, and remove any contaminated clothing.
2. Determine what was swallowed, when, and how much.
3. *For a responsive child,* call the national Poison Control Center (800-222-1222) immediately and follow their instructions.
4. *For an unresponsive child,* call 911 and provide basic life support (BLS) as needed.

Additional Care

- Put an unresponsive child who is breathing in the recovery position and be prepared for vomiting
- If a responsive child's mouth or lips are burned by a corrosive chemical, rinse the mouth with cold water (without swallowing)

ALERT

Swallowed Poison

Do not give syrup of ipecac to induce vomiting or activated charcoal unless told to do so by the Poison Control Center.

Food Poisoning

Food poisoning signs and symptoms may begin soon after eating or within a day.

When You See

- Nausea and vomiting, signs of abdominal pain or cramps
- Diarrhea, possibly with blood
- Headache, fever

Do This First

1. Have the child rest lying down.
2. Give the child fluids to drink.
3. Seek medical attention.

Additional Care

- Talk with the child's parents, who should check with others with whom the child has eaten recently

PREVENTING FOOD POISONING

To prevent food poisoning:

- Fully defrost frozen poultry and meat before cooking
- Fully cook poultry, meat, fish, and eggs to kill bacteria
- Do not keep cooked foods lukewarm a long time before serving
- Wash hands before preparing food; wash anytime after touching uncooked poultry

Poisonous Plants

If a child eats a part of a plant, unless you are absolutely certain the plant is nonpoisonous, call the Poison Control Center and give first aid as for swallowed poisons. Remove any plant parts remaining in the child's mouth. Take a piece of the plant with you to the telephone to help you describe it (**Figure 9-1**).

Alcohol

Even a small amount of alcohol consumed by a child, including the alcohol in many cough syrups, can lead to a medical emergency.

When You See

- Smell of alcohol about the child
- Flushed, moist face
- Slurred speech, staggering
- Nausea
- Changing levels of responsiveness

Do This First

1. Check for injuries or illness. Note that a child with uncontrolled diabetes may appear to be intoxicated.

2. *For a responsive intoxicated child:*
   a. Stay with the child and protect him or her from injury.
   b. Do not let the child lie down on his or her back.
3. *For an unresponsive intoxicated child:*
   a. If the child is breathing, position the child in the recovery position, preferably on the left side.
   b. Monitor the child's ABCs and provide BLS if necessary.
   c. Call 911 if the child's breathing is irregular, if seizures occur, or if the child cannot be roused (coma).

Drug Abuse or Overdose

A child under the influence of any drug or prescription medication may have a wide range of behaviors and symptoms, depending on the specific drug. In some cases it is impossible to know whether behavior or symptoms are caused by a drug or by an injury or sudden illness. Follow these general guidelines.

Figure 9-1 Plants that are poisonous when eaten.

When You See

- Very small or large pupils of the eye (see Figure 6-1)
- Stumbling, clumsiness, drowsiness, incoherent speech
- Difficulty breathing (very slow or fast)
- Irrational or violent behavior
- Changing levels of responsiveness
- Evidence of a suicide attempt

Do This First

1. Put an *unresponsive child* who is breathing in the recovery position, preferably on the left side, and give BLS as needed. Call 911.
2. For a *responsive child,* try to find out what drug the child took. If there is evidence of an overdose, call 911.
3. If symptoms are minor and you know the substance taken, call the Poison Control Center and follow their instructions.

Additional Care

- Monitor the child's condition while waiting for help
- Provide care for any condition that occurs (seizures, shock, cardiac arrest)

INHALED POISONS

Various gases and fumes may be present in different settings. Unless you know the specific treatment for inhaling a gas, care for a child with a suspected gas inhalation the same as for carbon monoxide.

Carbon Monoxide

Carbon monoxide is especially dangerous because it is invisible, odorless, and tasteless—and very lethal. Carbon monoxide may be present from motor vehicle exhaust, a faulty furnace or other heater, a fireplace or stove, or fire. Exposure to large amounts causes an immediate poisoning reaction. A slow or small leak may cause gradual poisoning with less dramatic symptoms. To prevent poisoning, carbon monoxide detectors should be used along with smoke detectors in appropriate locations.

When You See

- Headache
- Dizziness, lightheadedness, confusion, weakness
- Nausea, vomiting
- Signs of chest pain
- Convulsions
- Changing levels of responsiveness

Do This First

1. Immediately move the child into fresh air.
2. Call 911 even if the child starts to recover.
3. Monitor the child's ABCs and give BLS as needed.

Additional Care

- Put an unresponsive child who is breathing in the recovery position
- Loosen tight clothing around the neck or chest

Learning
Checkpoint (1)

1. Check off the common signs and symptoms of a swallowed poisoning.

___ **a.** Nausea

___ **b.** Uncontrolled shaking

___ **c.** Dizziness

___ **d.** Drowsiness

___ **e.** Red lips

___ **f.** Vomiting

___ **g.** Unresponsiveness

___ **h.** Hyperactivity

2. Name one action you would take for a child with food poisoning that you would not do for a child who swallowed a poison.

_____

3. True or False: Alcohol intoxication may put a child at risk for injury but is never a medical emergency.

4. True or False: You can tell when a child has taken a drug because he or she always has large (dilated) pupils.

5. The first thing to do for a child with carbon monoxide poisoning is:

a. Loosen tight clothing around the neck

b. Call 911

c. Move the child to fresh air

d. Start rescue breathing

6. You find a child unresponsive on the floor in a storeroom that should have been locked. A cabinet door is open, and the caps are off several bottles of cleaning products. Describe what actions you need to take.

_____

Poison Ivy, Oak, and Sumac

Contact with poison ivy, oak, and sumac plants causes an allergic skin reaction in about half of all children (**Figure 9-2**). Once the rash appears on the skin and has been washed, however, it cannot spread to anyone else. It is not a contagious condition but a reaction to a substance in the plant. It may take up to two weeks for the rash to heal.

When You See

- Redness and extreme itching occurring first
- Rash, blisters (may weep)
- Possible headache and fever

Do This First

1. Wash the area thoroughly with soap and water as soon as possible after contact.

2. For severe reactions or swelling on the face or groin area, the child needs medical attention.

3. Follow your childcare center's policy to treat itching with colloid oatmeal baths; a paste made of baking soda and water, calamine lotion, or topical hydrocortisone cream; and an oral antihistamine. Parental permission is required.

Additional Care

- Wash clothing and shoes (and pets) that contacted the plants to prevent further spread
- Childcare providers should inform the child's parents of an exposure to a poisonous plant, which may produce a rash hours or days later

ALERT

Poison Ivy/Oak/Sumac
Do not burn these poisonous plants to get rid of them as smoke also spreads the poisonous substance.

(a) Poison ivy

(b) Poison oak

(c) Poison sumac

Figure 9-2 Poisonous plants.

Learning
Checkpoint ②

1. True or False: Never put water on a site of contact with poison ivy because of the risk of spreading the rash further.

2. When should a child with a poison ivy or oak rash be seen by a healthcare provider?

_____

3. Which of the following can help reduce the itching of poison ivy?

   a. Hydrocortisone cream

   b. Rubbing alcohol

   c. A paste made with dishwasher detergent

   d. All of the above

BITES AND STINGS

Animal Bites

Animal bites cause a wound and carry the risk of rabies, which can be fatal without prompt treatment. Rabies should be suspected in cases of unprovoked attacks, strangely acting animals, or wild (nondomestic) animals.

When You See

- Any animal bite

Do This First

1. Wearing medical exam gloves, clean the wound with soap and water. Run water over the wound for five minutes (except for large wounds or severe bleeding).
2. Control the bleeding.
3. Cover the wound with a sterile dressing and bandage (see Chapter 3).
4. The child should see a healthcare provider or go to the emergency room right away. Follow your childcare center's policy.

Additional Care

- All animal bites must be reported to local animal control officers or police. The law requires certain procedures to be followed when rabies is a risk
- Check that the child's tetanus vaccination is up to date (see Chapter 3)

ALERT

Animal Bite

Do not try to catch any animal that may have rabies.

Human Bites

Because our mouths are full of germs, if a child is bitten by another child and the skin is broken, a wound infection may result.

When You See

- A human bite
- Open puncture wound
- Bleeding

Do This First

1. Wearing medical exam gloves, clean the wound with soap and water. Run water over wound for five minutes (except when bleeding severely).
2. Control bleeding.
3. Cover the wound with a sterile dressing and bandage (see Chapter 3).
4. The child should be seen by a healthcare provider or go to the emergency room right away. Follow your childcare center's policy.

Additional Care

- If any tissue has been bitten off, it should be taken with the child to the emergency room
- Check that the child's tetanus vaccination is up to date (see Chapter 3)

Snakebites

Poisonous snakes in North America include rattlesnakes, copperheads, water moccasins (cottonmouths), coral snakes, and exotic species kept in captivity. Rattlesnake bites cause most snakebite deaths. Treat all snakebites in children as potentially dangerous. Antivenin is often available in areas where snakebites are common. See Chapter 16 on preventing snakebites when children are outdoors.

When You See

- Puncture marks in skin
- Complaint of pain or burning at bite site
- Redness and swelling
- *Depending on snake species:* difficulty breathing, numbness or muscle paralysis, nausea and vomiting, blurred vision, drowsiness or confusion, weakness

Do This First

1. Have the child lie down and stay calm. (Do not move the child unless absolutely necessary.) Keep the bitten area immobile and below the level of the heart.
2. Call 911.
3. Wash the bite wound with soap and water.
4. Remove jewelry or tight clothing before swelling begins.

Additional Care

- Do not try to catch the snake, but note its appearance and describe it to the healthcare provider
- Stay with the child, monitor his or her ABCs, and give BLS if needed

ALERT

Snakebite
Do not put a tourniquet on a snakebite.

Pit Vipers

According to the Wilderness Medical Society, a child bitten by a pit viper, such as rattlesnake, may have one or two puncture wounds about one-half inch apart. Swelling can occur rapidly and involve the entire extremity. The child may become nauseated, vomit, sweat, and complain of weakness. Care involves removing the child and any bystanders from the snake. If possible, attempt to identify the snake's markings from a safe distance. Minimize movement of the child. Seek immediate medical attention. Gently wash the area with soap and water if available.

Spider Bites

Many types of spiders bite, but only the venom of the black widow and brown recluse spider is serious and sometimes fatal (**Figure 9-3**). The black widow often has a red hourglass-shaped marking on the underside of the abdomen. The brown recluse has a violin-shaped marking

(a) Black widow spider

(b) Brown recluse spider

Figure 9-3 Poisonous spiders.

on its back. An antivenin is available for black widow spider bites.

When You See

For black widow bite:

- Complaint of pain at bite site
- Red skin at site
- After 15 minutes to hours: sweating, nausea, stomach and muscle cramps, increased pain at site, dizziness or weakness, difficulty breathing

For brown recluse bite:

- Stinging sensation at site
- Over 8 to 48 hours: increasing pain, blistering at site, fever, chills, nausea or vomiting, joint pain, open sore at site

Do This First

1. If the child has difficulty breathing, call 911 and be prepared to give BLS. Call 911 immediately for a brown recluse spider bite.
2. Keep the bite area below the level of the heart.
3. Wash the area with soap and water.
4. Put ice or a cold pack on the bite area.

Additional Care

- Try to safely catch the spider to show the healthcare provider
- If 911 was not called, the child needs to be taken to the emergency room

Tick Bites

Tick bites are not poisonous but can transmit serious diseases like Rocky Mountain spotted fever or Lyme disease. The tick embeds its mouth parts in the skin and may remain for days (Figure 9-4).

When You See

- Tick embedded in skin

Do This First

1. Remove the tick by grasping it close to the skin with tweezers and pulling very gently until the tick finally lets go. Avoid pulling too hard or jerking, which may leave part of the tick in the skin (Figure 9-5).
2. Wash the area with soap and water.
3. Follow your childcare center's policy to put an antiseptic, such as rubbing alcohol, on the site followed by an antibiotic cream.

Additional Care

- Seek medical attention if a rash appears around the site or the child later experiences fever, chills, joint pain, or other flu-like symptoms

(a) Tick embedded in skin

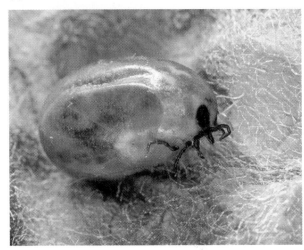

(b) Tick engorged

Figure 9-4 Tick bite.

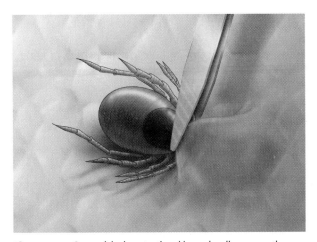

Figure 9-5 Grasp tick close to the skin and pull very gently.

Tick Removal

Do not try to remove an embedded tick by covering it with petroleum jelly, soaking it with bleach, burning it away with a hot pin or other object, or similar methods. These methods may result in part of the tick remaining embedded in the skin.

LYME DISEASE

Lyme disease, spread by ticks, has become a serious problem in many areas in the United States. Lyme disease is a bacterial infectious disease that first causes fever, chills, and other flu-like symptoms and later on may cause heart and neurological problems. Look for a bull's-eye rash that appears around the tick bite site 3 to 30 days later. If this rash, flu-like symptoms, or joint pain occurs after a tick bite, the child needs medical attention (**Figure 9-6**).

Bee and Wasp Stings

Bee, wasp, and other insect stings are common in children playing outdoors. These stings are not poisonous but can cause life-threatening allergic reactions in children with severe allergies to them (see Chapter 4 on anaphylactic shock).

When You See

- Complaints of pain, burning, or itching at sting site
- Redness, swelling
- Stinger possibly still in skin

Do This First

1. Remove the stinger from the skin by scraping it away gently with a credit card or knife blade. Call 911 if the child is known to be allergic to stings (see Chapter 4).

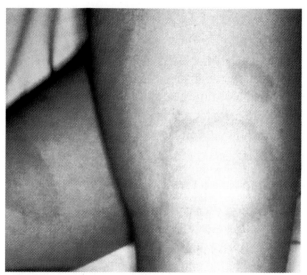

Figure 9-6 Lyme disease bull's-eye rash.

2. Wash the area with soap and water.
3. Put ice or a cold pack on the sting site.
4. Watch the child for 30 minutes for any signs or symptoms of allergic reaction (difficulty breathing, swelling in other areas, anxiety, nausea or vomiting); call 911 and treat for shock.

Additional Care

- A mixture of baking soda and water or calamine lotion may be applied to the sting area to reduce the discomfort
- Follow your childcare center's policy for using an over-the-counter oral antihistamine to help reduce discomfort or calamine to reduce itching. Parental permission is required.

Insect Sting in Mouth

Have the child suck on ice to reduce swelling. Call 911 if breathing becomes difficult.

Scorpion Stings

Scorpion stings are treated similarly to spider bites. Of the different types of scorpions in the American Southwest, some are more poisonous than others and could be dangerous, especially for young children. Antivenin may be available in some areas (**Figure 9-7**).

When You See

- The scorpion sting with its tail
- Complaints of severe burning pain at sting site, later numbness, tingling
- Nausea, vomiting
- Difficulty swallowing
- Possible convulsions, coma

Do This First

1. Call 911 if the child has trouble breathing.
2. Monitor the child's ABCs and give BLS as needed.
3. Carefully wash the sting area.
4. Put ice or a cold pack on the area.
5. Seek urgent medical attention.

Additional Care

- Keep the child still

Marine Bites and Stings

Biting marine animals include sharks, barracudas, and eels. Give this first aid for marine bites:

1. Stop the bleeding.
2. Care for shock.
3. Summon help from lifeguards.
4. Call 911.

Figure 9-7 Scorpion.

Stinging marine life include jellyfish, Portuguese man-of-war, corals, and anemones. Give this first aid for marine animal stings:

1. Scrape off any tentacles on skin with a credit card or stick, or pick them off with tweezers or pliers.
2. Apply vinegar to the affected area.
3. Seek medical attention.

To care for stingray puncture wounds:

1. Relieve the pain by immersing the injured part in hot water for 30 minutes. Make sure the water is not so hot that it causes a burn.
2. Wash the wound with soap and water.
3. Seek medical attention.

Learning
Checkpoint (3)

1. To minimize the risk of rabies from an animal bite, take which action?

  a. See a healthcare provider immediately

  b. See a healthcare provider if the child experiences heavy salivation 5 to 7 days after the bite

  c. Capture the animal and take it to a veterinarian for examination

  d. Soak the wound area with rubbing alcohol

2. Why can a human bite lead to a serious medical condition?

_____

3. List three key actions to take for a child who has been bitten by a snake.

_____

4. In which situation should you put a tourniquet on a child's leg?

  a. Any snakebite to the leg

  b. Any spider bite to the leg

  c. Any bite or sting that causes bleeding

  d. None of the above

5. Check off situations in which you should call 911 for a spider bite:

___ **a.** All spider bites   ___ **d.** If there is any pain at the bite site

___ **b.** Any spider bite in diabetic child   ___ **e.** If the child has trouble breathing

___ **c.** Any brown recluse spider bite   ___ **f.** If you have no ice to put on the bite

6. A tick is best removed from the skin using _____.

7. A bee's stinger can be removed from the skin using _____.

8. A child is stung by a honeybee in the play yard of your childcare center. As she tells you about this, you see that her face is turning red, the skin around her eyes and mouth looks puffy, and she seems short of breath. What are the most important actions to take first? Why?

_____

Chapter

10 Heat and Cold Emergencies

C old or hot environments can cause medical problems for children if they are not protected from temperature extremes. Often cold- and heat-related injuries begin gradually, but if a child remains exposed to an extreme temperature, an emergency can develop. Untreated, it can lead to serious injury or death.

COLD INJURIES

Exposure to cold temperatures can cause either localized freezing of skin and other tissues (**frostnip** or **frostbite**) or lowering of the whole body's temperature (**hypothermia**). Frostbite occurs when the temperature is 32 degrees Fahrenheit or colder. Hypothermia can occur at much warmer temperatures if the body is unprotected, especially if the child is wet, exposed a long time, or unable to restore body heat because of a medical condition.

Frostbite

Frostbite is the freezing of skin or deeper tissues. It usually happens to exposed skin areas on the head or face, hands, or feet. Wind chill increases the risk of frostbite. Severe frostbite kills tissue and can result in gangrene and having to amputate the body part (**Figure 10-1**).

Frostnip is a less serious freezing of superficial skin areas, but it may progress to frostbite and become serious.

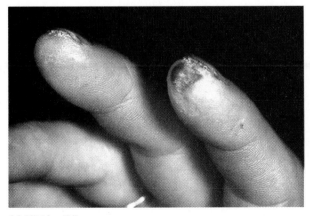

(a) Mild frostbite

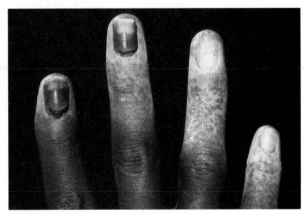

(b) Severe frostbite

Figure 10-1 Frostbite.

When You See

- Skin looks waxy and white, gray, yellow, or bluish
- The area is numb or feels tingly or aching
- With severe frostbite:
  - The area feels hard
  - May become painless
  - After warming, the area becomes swollen and may blister

Do This First

1. Move the child to a warm environment. Gently hold the frostbitten area with your hands to warm it. (A child with frostbitten hands can warm them in his or her armpits.) Check the child also for hypothermia.
2. Remove any tight clothing or jewelry from the area.
3. Put dry gauze or fluffy cloth between frostbitten fingers or toes (**Figure 10-2**).
4. Obtain medical attention as soon as possible.
5. Additionally for severe frostbite:
   a. Warm the frostbitten area in lukewarm, not hot, water for at least 20 minutes or up to 45 minutes (**Figure 10-3**).
   b. Protect the area from being touched or rubbed by clothing or objects.
   c. Elevate the area if possible to reduce swelling.

Additional Care

- Follow your childcare center's policy for giving acetaminophen or ibuprofen for pain (parental permission required)
- Give the child a warm liquid to drink
- Prevent the area from refreezing

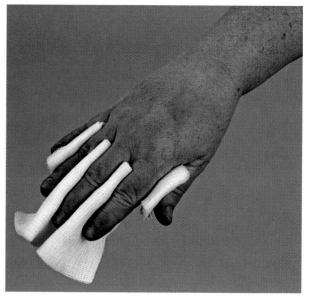

Figure 10-2 Protect between frostbitten fingers or toes.

104°F

Figure 10-3 Warm the frostbitten fingers or toes.

Hypothermia

When a child's body cannot make heat as fast as it loses it in a cold environment, the child develops hypothermia. In hypothermia, the body temperature drops below 95 degrees Fahrenheit. Hypothermia can occur whenever and wherever the child feels cold, including indoors in poorly heated areas. It may occur gradually or quickly, especially with a wind chill or if the child is wet.

ALERT

Frostbite

Do not rub frostbitten skin because this can damage the skin.
Do not rewarm frostbitten skin if it may be frozen again, which could worsen the injury.
Do not use a fire, heat lamp, hot water bottle, or heating pad to warm the area.
After rewarming, be careful not to break blisters.

Learning
Checkpoint ①

1. True or False: Rubbing frostbitten fingers is the best way to warm them.

2. Frostbitten skin usually has what color(s)?

_____

3. A child who has been playing in the snow comes to you complaining of being very cold. He has lost his hat and his ears are white and hard and he says he has no feeling in them. Describe three actions to take for this child's frostbite.

_____

FACTS ABOUT HYPOTHERMIA

- Hypothermia occurs more easily in someone who is ill.
- A child immersed in cold water loses body heat 30 times faster than in cool air.
- A child in cold water is more likely to die from hypothermia than to drown.
- Children in cardiac arrest after immersion in cold water have been resuscitated after a long time underwater—don't give up!

When You See

- Shivering may be uncontrollable (but stops in severe hypothermia)
- Child seems apathetic, confused, or irrational; may be belligerent
- Lethargy, clumsy movements, drowsiness
- Pale, cool skin—even under clothing
- Slow breathing
- Changing levels of responsiveness

Do This First

1. With an unresponsive child, check the ABCs and provide BLS as needed. Call 911 for any child with hypothermia.

2. Quickly get the child out of the cold and remove any wet clothing. Handle the child gently.

3. Have the child lie down, and cover him or her with blankets or warm clothing. If necessary, warm the child with your own body (Figure 10-4).

Additional Care

- Stay with the child until help arrives.

Hypothermia

Do not immerse a child with hypothermia in hot water or use direct heat (hot water bottle, heat lamp, heating pad), because rapid warming can cause heart problems.

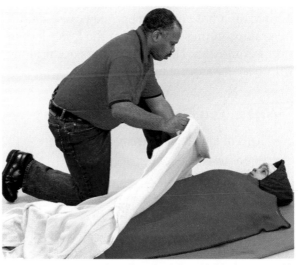

Figure 10-4 Warm a hypothermia victim with blankets, not with hot water.

Learning
Checkpoint ②

1. True or False: Hypothermia occurs only when the air temperature is below freezing.

2. True or False: A child with hypothermia who is generating heat by shivering still needs first aid and warming.

3. A child with mild hypothermia needs to be warmed. It will help to:

a. Have the child take off his or her outer clothes and sit close to a fireplace or heater

b. Send the child to a hot shower

c. Remove the child's damp clothing and warm him or her with a blanket

d. Any of the above will be effective

HEAT EMERGENCIES

Heat illnesses can result when children become overheated in a hot environment:

- *Heat cramps* are the least serious and usually first to occur
- *Heat exhaustion* develops when the body becomes dehydrated in a hot environment
- *Heatstroke,* with a seriously high body temperature, may develop from heat exhaustion. It is a medical emergency and, if untreated, usually causes death

Heat Cramps

Activity in a hot environment may cause painful cramps in muscles, often in the lower legs or stomach muscles. Heat cramps may occur along with heat exhaustion and heatstroke.

When You See
- Signs of muscle pain, cramping, spasms
- Heavy sweating

Do This First
1. Have the child stop the activity and sit quietly in a cool place.
2. Give a sports drink or water.

Additional Care
- For abdominal cramps, continue resting in a comfortable position
- For leg cramps, have the child stretch the muscle by extending the leg and flexing the ankle. Apply pressure to the cramped area.

Heat Exhaustion

Activity in a hot environment usually causes heavy sweating, which may lead to dehydration and depletion of salt and electrolytes in the body if the child does not get enough fluids. This situation could occur, for example, with a prolonged sports activity. Unrelieved, heat exhaustion may develop into heatstroke, a true medical emergency.

Learning
Checkpoint ③

1. True or False: For abdominal heat cramps, the best care is vigorous massage and stomach kneading.

2. To treat heat cramps:

   a. Immerse the child in a bathtub of cold water

   b. Give the child a sports drink or water to drink

   c. Keep the child very active until the cramp works itself out

   d. Do not let the child eat or drink anything

3. Heat cramps can also occur with heat _____ and heat _____.

When You See

- Heavy sweating
- Thirst
- Fatigue
- Heat cramps

Later signs and symptoms:
- Headache, dizziness
- Nausea, vomiting

Do This First

1. Move the child out of the heat to rest in a cool place. Loosen or remove unnecessary clothing.
2. Give a sports drink or water to drink.
3. Raise the feet 8 to 12 inches.
4. Cool the child by putting wet cloths on the forehead and body or sponging the skin with cool water (**Figure 10-5**).

Additional Care

- Seek medical care if the child's condition worsens or does not improve within 30 minutes

Heat Exhaustion

Do not give a child with heat exhaustion or heatstroke salt tablets. Use a sports drink instead (if the child is awake and alert).
Do not give liquids containing caffeine.
If the child is lethargic, nauseous, or vomiting, do not give any liquids.

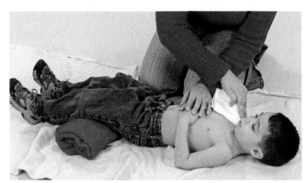

Figure 10-5 Cool a child with heat exhaustion.

Learning
Checkpoint ④

1. True or False: Give salt tablets to older children who have both heat cramps and heat exhaustion.

2. The problem of heat exhaustion begins when someone in a hot environment is not getting enough _____.

3. List two ways to cool a child with heat exhaustion.

_____

Heatstroke

Heatstroke is a life-threatening emergency that is more common during hot summer periods. It may develop slowly over several days or more rapidly in someone engaged in strenuous activity in the heat. A child may be dehydrated and not sweating when heatstroke gradually develops, or may be sweating heavily from exertion. Heatstroke causes a body temperature of 104 degrees Fahrenheit or higher and is different from heat exhaustion in these ways:

- In heatstroke the child's skin is flushed and feels very hot to the touch; in heat exhaustion the skin may be pale and clammy
- In heatstroke the child becomes very confused and irrational and may become unresponsive or have convulsions; in heat exhaustion the child is dizzy or disoriented

When You See

- Skin flushed and very hot to the touch, sweating may have stopped
- Fast breathing
- Headache, dizziness, confusion
- Irrational behavior
- Possible convulsions or unresponsiveness

Do This First

1. Call 911.
2. Move the child to a cool place and monitor his or her ABCs.

3. Remove outer clothing.
4. Cool the child quickly with any means at hand:
  - Wrap the child in a wet sheet and keep it wet
  - Sponge the child with cold water
  - Spray the skin with water and then fan the area
  - Put ice bags or cold packs beside the neck, armpits, and groin (**Figure 10-6**)

Additional Care

- Stay with the child and be prepared to give BLS if needed
- Put an unresponsive child who is breathing in the recovery position
- Protect a child having convulsions from injury (see Chapter 8)

Figure 10-6 Cool a child with heatstroke.

Heatstroke

A child with heatstroke should not take pain relievers or salt tablets.

Learning Checkpoint ⑤

1. True or False:　It is safe to let a child with heatstroke go home after you have given first aid and cooled his or her body down to 100 degrees Fahrenheit, as long as the child is feeling better.

2. In what situation should you call 911 for a child with heatstroke?

_____

3. Describe how a child with heatstroke may behave differently from how he or she usually behaves.

_____

4. On a very hot day you are scheduled to take a group of children to play soccer.

a. To make sure none of the children experiences a heat emergency, what things should you make sure are present at the soccer field?

b. A parent volunteer is assisting you in supervising the children's soccer game. What would you tell this parent about how to prevent heat emergencies? What signs and symptoms of a potential problem should you watch out for?

11 Common Minor Childhood Problems and Injuries

The childhood problems and injuries described in this chapter are seldom emergencies. Yet these are common problems that cause pain, discomfort, or other problems for children, and caregivers should know the first aid steps to take.

OBJECT IN EAR

Small children often put things in their ears, or an insect may crawl in while the child is sleeping. A child may be fussing with the ear or tell you there is something in it.

When You See

- Child is bothered by ear
- Child feels something moving in ear

Do This First

1. Look in the ear to see the object, but do not try to remove it. Only a healthcare provider should remove an object from the ear.
2. If you see or know an insect is in the ear, gently pour lukewarm water into the ear to try to float it out. If it does not come out, the child should see a healthcare provider.

Additional Care

- Reassure the child

Action for parents:
- Take the child to a healthcare provider for removal of an object or insect that does not come out

ALERT

Object in Ear

Never insert tweezers or anything else in a child's ear in an attempt to remove an object or insect, because of the risk of injury or pushing it farther in. See a healthcare provider.

OBJECT IN NOSE

A young child may have an object in the nose for some time before telling caregivers.

When You See

- Noisy or difficult breathing through nose
- Nasal discharge on one side
- Child may pick at nose with fingers
- Possible swelling of nose

Do This First

1. Look in the nose to see object, but do not try to remove it. Only a healthcare provider should remove an object from the nose, because of the risk of pushing it in farther.
2. Tell child to breathe through the mouth.

Additional Care

- Calm and reassure the child

Action for parents:

- Take child to a healthcare provider for removal of the object

Object in Nose

Except with an older child skilled at blowing his or her nose, do not have the child try to expel an object from the nose by blowing it out. A young child may instead suck it in deeper.

SWALLOWED OBJECT

If the swallowed object is small and smooth, like a coin or button, it will usually pass through the child's system easily and safely. Any object that can dissolve may be poisonous, however (see Chapter 9). Be sure the object was swallowed and is not lodged in the windpipe, producing the signs of choking (see Chapter 2).

When You See

- You see or the child tells you he or she swallowed something

Do This First

1. Talk to the child to confirm what was swallowed.
2. With small, smooth, nonpoisonous objects, no action may be needed.
3. With objects that are larger or pointed or have rough edges, the child should see a healthcare provider. Do not give the child anything to eat or drink.

Additional Care

Actions for parents:

- Take the child to a healthcare provider for a large or sharp object
- Call a healthcare provider if there is any question about the safety of the swallowed object
- Observe the child for three to four days, and call the healthcare provider for any abdominal pain

Swallowed Object

Do not try to induce vomiting or give a laxative to a child who swallows an object. Call a healthcare provider for advice if unsure about the safety of the swallowed object.

BUMP ON THE HEAD

Children often fall or run into things and bump their heads. With a more severe impact there may be bleeding or a more serious head injury (see Chapter 3 and Chapter 6). This section describes care for a minor bump not involving bleeding. The pain of such a bump usually does not last long.

When You See

- Child crying, holding head
- Swollen bump, often a large "goose egg"

Do This First

1. Calm and reassure the child.
2. Hold a covered ice or cold pack on the bump to minimize swelling and pain.
3. Monitor the child for any signs of a more serious injury. Call a healthcare provider immediately if the child becomes unresponsive or unusually lethargic, has enlarged pupils, vomits repeatedly, becomes very pale, or sweats heavily.

Additional Care

Action for parents:

• Continue to watch the child for development of any additional symptoms, and call a healthcare provider immediately if so

SPLINTERS

Wooden splinters in a child are usually only a minor problem (**Figure 11-1**).

When You See

• A splinter in the child's skin

Do This First

1. Wash the area with soap and water.

2. Sterilize a pair of tweezers with alcohol or disinfectant and dry them. Grasp the splinter close to the skin and pull it out at the same angle.
3. Squeeze the skin around the area to promote bleeding to flush out the wound.
4. Wash the area again and apply a local antiseptic, if allowed. Cover the wound with an adhesive bandage.

Additional Care

• If the splinter is too deep to remove, apply antiseptic and bandage and wait for the splinter to work itself out in a day or two.

Action for parents:

• Talk to a healthcare provider if a part of the splinter remains beneath the skin

ALERT

Splinter
Do not use a needle or knife to try to dig out a splinter beneath the skin.

TONGUE BITE

When a child bites his or her tongue, there may be significant bleeding at first. The situation usually looks scarier than it is.

(a) Grasp a splinter close to the skin.

(b) Squeeze the skin around the area to promote bleeding.

Figure 11-1 Removing a splinter.

Learning
Checkpoint ①

1. True or False: You can gently sweep an object out of a child's ear with something like a cotton-tipped swab as long as it is not sharp.

2. When should a child see a healthcare provider for a foreign object in the nose?

_____

3. True or False: It is essential for parents to check the child's bowel movements to ensure he or she passes any swallowed object.

4. List at least four signs of a possible serious head injury for which a child with a bump on the head should see a healthcare provider.

_____

5. What should you not do when removing a splinter?

a. Wash the area first

b. Grasp the splinter close to the skin with tweezers

c. Use a needle to dig out a splinter below the skin

d. Squeeze the area to promote a little bleeding after removal

When You See

- Child's tongue bleeding

Do This First

1. Have child spit out the blood rather than swallow it.
2. Rinse mouth with cold water.
3. Wearing gloves, press a piece of clean gauze on the wound to control the bleeding.

Additional Care

- A cold pack on the lips or tongue may help reduce pain and swelling
- Do not let child eat or drink anything for a while

Action for parents:
- Call a healthcare provider if the bleeding does not stop soon or the wound seems deep

FINGERNAIL INJURY

When a child smashes a finger, the fingernail may be partly or completely torn away, or there may be bleeding beneath the nail. The injury usually looks worse than it is, however, and except in very severe injuries the nail will grow back over four to sixteen weeks.

When You See

- Bleeding around and under a fingernail or toenail
- The nail torn partly or completely away

Do This First

1. Check that the child can move the finger or joints; a possible fracture should be seen by a healthcare provider.
2. Gently wash or rinse the nail area to clean it.

3. Leave the damaged nail in place.

4. Use an ice or cold pack to reduce swelling and pain.

Additional Care

- Follow your center's policy for giving children's acetaminophen or ibuprofen for pain if needed (parental permission required)

Actions for parents:

- Call a healthcare provider if the pressure of blood trapped under the nail causes pain
- Keep the fingernail bandaged as long as it is painful or if a ragged edge may catch and tear the remaining nail

LOSING A BABY TOOTH

New parents and caregivers sometimes worry about children losing their baby teeth and swallowing or choking on them. In reality this very rarely happens, although it may be a concern if a child's tooth is knocked out by a blow. In this case, be sure the tooth is not caught in the child's throat; if so, give first aid for choking (see Chapter 2).

If a baby tooth that was not loose is knocked out, the child's dentist should be called, because in some cases the dentist may want to reimplant the tooth. If so, control bleeding in the child and care for the tooth (see Chapter 3).

When You See

- A child loses a baby tooth that was loose

Do This First

1. Have child spit out the blood rather than swallow it.

2. Rinse mouth with cold water.

3. Wearing gloves, put a rolled or folded piece of clean gauze over the tooth socket and apply gentle pressure to control bleeding.

Additional Care

- Do not let child eat or drink anything for a while
- Save the tooth for the child's parents

BLISTERS

Blisters usually occur because of friction on the skin, such as if a child's shoe rubs the back of the ankle or heel. They can be painful and may become infected after breaking. Burns may cause a different kind of blister (see Chapter 5).

When You See

- A raised, fluid-filled blister, often surrounded by red skin

Do This First

1. Wash the blister and surrounding area with soap and water. Rinse and gently pat dry.

2. Cover the blister with an adhesive bandage big enough that the gauze pad covers the whole blister. Bandages with an adhesive strip on all four sides are best because they keep the area cleaner if the blister breaks.

Additional Care

- Prevent continued friction in the area

ALERT

Blister
Never deliberately break a blister.
This could lead to infection.

Learning
Checkpoint ②

1. Name two situations in which a child who has bitten his or her tongue should see a healthcare provider.

_____   _____

2. True or False: If an injured fingernail is hanging on to the finger by only one edge, you should pull it off to allow better healing and growth of a new nail.

3. Describe how to stop the bleeding when a child loses a baby tooth.

_____

4. True or false: Because blisters need air to heal, bandage them with one side of the bandage open.

12 Child Abuse and Neglect

Child abuse and neglect are major problems in our society. Over 2,000 children a day are discovered to be victims of child abuse or neglect. Each week, child protective service agencies throughout the United States receive more than 50,000 reports of suspected child abuse or neglect. Every year over 800,000 children are found to have been victims of abuse or neglect. About two-thirds of these children are experiencing neglect, meaning a caretaker failed to provide for their basic needs. Almost 20% are found to have been physically abused, and about 10% sexually abused. About 8% are victims of emotional abuse, which includes criticizing, rejecting, or refusing to nurture a child. An average of three children die every day as a result of child abuse or neglect.

Childcare workers, teachers, and parents all need to understand the nature of this problem and what they can do for children being abused.

Much of the information in this chapter comes from the National Clearinghouse on Child Abuse and Neglect Information, of the U.S. Department of Health & Human Services Administration for Children & Families. Additional information is available at this agency's web site: http://nccanch.acf.hhs.gov.

WHY ABUSE OCCURS

All the causes of child abuse and neglect are not fully understood, but several risk factors have been identified. When there are multiple risk factors present, the risk is greater. These risk factors include:

- Lack of preparation or knowledge for parenting

- Financial or other environmental stressors
- Difficulty in relationships
- Depression or other mental health problems

Parents may lack an understanding of their children's developmental stages and hold unreasonable expectations for their abilities. They also may be unaware of alternatives to corporal punishment or how to discipline their children most effectively at each age. Parents also may lack knowledge of the health, hygiene, and nutritional needs of their children. These circumstances, combined with the challenges of raising children, can result in otherwise well-intentioned parents causing their children harm or neglecting their needs.

Abuse may also result from uncontrolled emotional states. A particular problem, for example, is **shaken baby syndrome,** in which a parent or caregiver, including babysitters and childcare workers, becomes frustrated with a crying infant and shakes the infant. Such shaking causes the infant's head to flop around and may cause severe brain injury, spinal injury, or death. Everyone who cares for infants needs to understand this problem and to learn to control their emotions when frustrated by the crying of a child.

WHO IS ABUSED

Any child may be abused. Boys and girls are almost equally likely to experience neglect and physical abuse. Girls are four times more likely to experience sexual abuse. Children of all races and ethnicities and all socioeconomic levels experience abuse.

Children of all ages experience abuse and neglect, but younger children are most vulnerable. Infants under one year old account for nearly one-half of deaths resulting from child abuse and neglect, and about 85% of children who die are younger than six years of age.

Mothers acting alone are responsible for almost half the cases of neglect and about one-third of the cases of physical abuse. Fathers acting alone are responsible for about one-fourth of cases of sexual abuse, and unrelated perpetrators about one-third of cases of sexual abuse. In about 80% of cases of sexual abuse, the perpetrator is known by the child. Often sexual abuse occurs in a pattern rather than a single incident.

TYPES OF ABUSE AND NEGLECT

The **Federal Child Abuse Prevention and Treatment Act,** amended by the Keeping Children and Families Safe Act of 2003, defines child abuse and neglect as, at minimum:

- Any recent act or failure to act on the part of a parent or caretaker which results in death, serious physical or emotional harm, sexual abuse or exploitation; or
- An act or failure to act which presents an imminent risk of serious harm.

Each state, however, has its own laws and exact definitions of child abuse and neglect, which are typically based on the national standard. Most states recognize four major types of maltreatment: neglect, physical abuse, sexual abuse, and emotional abuse. Although any of these types may occur separately, they are more often combined. For example, a physically abused child is often emotionally abused as well, and a sexually abused child also may be neglected.

Neglect

Neglect is failure to provide for a child's basic needs, including these forms of neglect:

- *Physical neglect.* Failure to provide necessary food or shelter, or a lack of appropriate supervision.
- *Medical neglect.* Failure to provide necessary medical or mental health treatment.
- *Educational neglect.* Failure to educate a child or attend to special education needs.
- *Emotional neglect.* Inattention to a child's emotional needs, failure to provide psychological care, or permitting the child to use alcohol or other drugs.

These situations do not always mean a child is willfully neglected, however. Sometimes cultural values, community standards, and poverty may be contributing factors. The family may need information or assistance. When a family fails to use information and resources, and the child's health or safety is at risk, then child welfare intervention may be required.

Physical Abuse

Physical abuse is physical injury (ranging from minor bruises to severe fractures or death) as a result of punching, beating, kicking, biting, shaking, throwing, stabbing, choking, hitting (with a hand, stick, strap, or other object), burning, or otherwise harming a child. These injuries are considered abuse regardless of whether the caretaker intended to hurt the child.

Sexual Abuse

Sexual abuse includes any kind of sexual activity by a parent or caretaker, such as fondling a child's genitals, penetration, incest, rape, sodomy, indecent exposure, or exploitation through prostitution or the production of pornographic materials.

Emotional Abuse

Emotional abuse is a pattern of behavior that impairs a child's emotional development or sense of self-worth. This may include constant criticism, threats, or rejection, as well as withholding love, support, or guidance. Emotional abuse is often difficult to prove, and government agencies often cannot intervene without evidence of harm to the child. Emotional abuse is almost always present when other types of abuse occur.

RESULTS OF ABUSE AND NEGLECT

Abuse and neglect have short- and long-term consequences that may include brain damage, developmental delays, learning disorders, problems forming relationships, aggressive behavior, and depression. Survivors of child abuse and neglect may also be at greater risk for problems later in life, such as low academic achievement, drug use, teen pregnancy, and criminal behavior.

SIGNS OF ABUSE AND NEGLECT

The first step in helping abused or neglected children is learning to recognize the signs of abuse and neglect. A single sign does not prove child abuse is occurring, but when signs appear repeatedly or in combination, you should consider the possibility of child abuse.

General Signs of Abuse

Behavioral signs may signal abuse or neglect long before any physical changes occur in a child. The following behaviors may suggest the possibility of child abuse or neglect:

The child:
- Has sudden changes in behavior or school performance
- Has not received help for physical or medical problems brought to the parents' attention
- Has learning problems or difficulty concentrating unrelated to specific physical or psychological causes
- Is always watchful, as though preparing for something bad to happen
- Lacks adult supervision
- Is overly compliant, passive, or withdrawn
- Comes to school or other activities early, stays late, and does not want to go home

The parent:
- Shows little concern for the child
- Denies the existence of—or blames the child for—the child's problems in school or at home
- Asks teachers or other caretakers to use harsh physical discipline if the child misbehaves
- Sees the child as entirely bad, worthless, or burdensome
- Demands a level of physical or academic performance the child cannot achieve
- Looks primarily to the child for care, attention, and satisfaction of emotional needs

The parent and child:
- Rarely touch or look at each other
- Consider their relationship entirely negative
- Say they do not like each other

Signs of Neglect

The child:
- Is frequently absent from school
- Begs or steals food or money
- Lacks needed medical or dental care, immunizations, or glasses
- Is consistently dirty and has severe body odor
- Lacks sufficient clothing for the weather

- Abuses alcohol or other drugs
- Says there is no one at home to provide care

The parent or other adult caregiver:
- Appears indifferent to the child
- Seems apathetic or depressed
- Behaves irrationally or in a bizarre manner
- Is abusing alcohol or other drugs

See the box below for specific signs of the different types of abuse.

SIGNS OF ABUSE

Signs of Physical Abuse
The child:
- Has unexplained scalding or burns, rope burns, lacerations, bites, bruises, broken bones, or black eyes
- Has fading bruises or other marks after an absence from school or childcare
- Seems frightened of parents and protests or cries when it is time to go home
- Shrinks at the approach of adults
- Reports being injured by a parent or another adult caregiver
- Appears withdrawn or depressed and cries often—or is aggressive and disruptive
- Seems tired often and complains of frequent nightmares

The parent or other adult caregiver:
- Offers conflicting, unconvincing, or no explanation for the child's injury
- Describes the child with words such as "evil" or other negative terms
- Uses harsh physical discipline with the child
- Is known to have a history of abuse as a child

Signs of Sexual Abuse
The child:
- Has difficulty walking or sitting
- Suddenly refuses to change clothing when necessary or to participate in physical activities
- Reports nightmares or bedwetting
- Experiences a sudden change in appetite
- Demonstrates bizarre, sophisticated, or unusual sexual knowledge or behavior
- Becomes pregnant or contracts a venereal disease, particularly if under age 14
- Runs away from home
- Reports sexual abuse by a parent or other adult caregiver
- Seems afraid of a particular person or being alone with that person

The parent or other adult caregiver:
- Is unduly protective of the child or severely limits the child's contact with other children, especially of the opposite sex
- Is secretive and isolated
- Is jealous or controlling with family members

Signs of Emotional Abuse
The child:
- Is extreme in behavior, such as overly compliant or demanding, extremely passive or aggressive
- Acts either inappropriately like an adult (such as parenting other children) or inappropriately like an infant (such as frequently rocking or head-banging)
- Has delayed physical or emotional development
- Has attempted suicide
- Demonstrates a lack of attachment to the parent

The parent or other adult caregiver:
- Constantly blames, belittles, or berates the child
- Seems unconcerned about the child and refuses to consider offers of help for the child's problems
- Overtly rejects the child

HELPING AN ABUSED CHILD

Parents or other caregivers who abuse or neglect a child need help. Programs are available in most communities to provide professional help.

Childcare workers, teachers, and other caregivers should not, however, try to talk to suspected abusers in an effort to get them to seek help. Almost always the abuser will deny the problem, and the situation may become worse than if you had said nothing. Instead, the single most important thing you can do, if you suspect a child is being abused or neglected, is report it to the proper authorities. Your report will help protect the child and get help for the family.

Reporting Abuse

If you care for children as part of your job, you may be legally required to report suspected cases of child abuse or neglect. State laws vary in the specifics of who must make a report and to what agency. If this is required in your job, follow your employer's policy. For example, you may be required to speak to your supervisor about your suspicion before making a report.

The law provides ways for private citizens to report suspected abuse or neglect as well, and it is important for the child's welfare that you do this even if not required to do so by your employer. Contact your local child protective services agency or police department. For more information about where and how to file a report, call the Childhelp USA® National Child Abuse Hotline (1-800-4-A-CHILD).

When you call to report child abuse, you will be asked for specific information, which may include:

- The child's name
- The suspected perpetrator's name (if known)
- A description of what you have seen or heard
- The names of any other people having knowledge of the abuse
- Your name and phone number

Your name will not be given to the family of the child you suspect is being abused or neglected. If you are making the report as a private citizen, you may request to make the report anonymously, but your report may be considered more credible and can be more helpful to the child protective services agency if you give your name.

Remember: Your suspicion of child abuse or neglect is enough to make a report. You do not have to provide proof. Almost every state has a law to protect people who make good-faith reports of child abuse from prosecution or liability.

What Happens When a Report Is Made

When a report is made it will first be screened by the agency. If the agency determines there is enough credible information to indicate that maltreatment may have occurred or is at risk of occurring, an investigation will be conducted. Depending on the potential severity of the situation, investigators may respond within hours or days. They may speak with the child, the parents, and other people in contact with the child, such as healthcare providers, teachers, or childcare providers.

If the investigator feels the child is at risk of harm, the family may be referred to any of various programs to reduce the risk of future maltreatment. These may include mental health care, medical care, parenting skills classes, employment assistance, and support services such as financial or housing assistance. In rare cases where the child's safety cannot be ensured, the child may be removed from the home.

The best way to prevent child abuse and neglect is to support families and provide parents with the skills and resources they need. Prevention efforts build on family strengths. Through activities such as parent education, home visitation, and parent support groups, many families are able to find the support they need to stay together and care for their children in their homes and communities. Prevention efforts help parents develop their parenting skills, understand the benefits of nonviolent discipline techniques, and understand and meet their child's emotional, physical, and developmental needs.

First Aid for an Apparently Abused Child

If you suspect a child in your care is being abused or neglected, do not confront the parents or ask the child direct questions about abuse. If the child needs first aid for an illness or injury, provide it as you would for any child, following the standard guidelines for providing care. Follow your facility's guidelines for documenting the care and any additional actions. If the child tells you an injury was caused by a parent or other adult, include this information when making your report.

Learning Checkpoint ①

1. True or False: Parents or others who abuse or neglect their children always intend to harm the child.

2. True or False: Young children are more vulnerable to child abuse or neglect.

3. True or False: It is important to gather proof of abuse or neglect before reporting the case.

4. True or False: In some states childcare workers are required to report suspected cases of abuse or neglect.

13 Common Childhood Illnesses

Children frequently experience common illnesses because their immune systems are not yet fully developed and because infections spread among children quickly in indoor settings such as schools and childcare centers. Fortunately, most childhood illnesses are not serious, although a few can become medical emergencies. The spread of viral and bacterial illness can be minimized with good ventilation and preventive practices such as frequent handwashing, early recognition and treatment of illness, and keeping a sick child home from school or childcare. Whenever a child is suspected of having an infectious disease, be sure to follow universal precautions to prevent transmission of the disease to others (see Chapter 1).

COLDS

Common colds generally last five to ten days. Colds are transmitted from one person to another, not caught by getting cold or wet. Colds are most contagious during the first few days. Cold medicines do not cure or shorten colds but may offer some relief from symptoms.

Causes include:
- Respiratory viruses

When You See
- Sore throat, coughing
- Sneezing, stuffy or running nose
- Red, watery eyes
- Headache, body aches and pains
- Fever

Do This First
1. Treat symptoms with children's cough medicine and decongestants if needed (not aspirin). Parental permission required
2. Use a cool-mist humidifier or vaporizer to minimize congestion.
3. Give plenty of fluids.
4. Do not let child share toys or eating utensils.

Additional Care
- Teach child to blow nose, use tissues when sneezing, and cover mouth when coughing

Actions for parents:
- Call a healthcare provider if fever becomes high or prolonged, if ears hurt, if the child is breathing rapidly, or if sore throat becomes severe.
- Child may attend school or childcare when a fever is under control and the child does not have nausea or diarrhea

SORE THROAT

Sore throat may be a symptom of a cold or something as simple as sleeping with the mouth open, or a more serious condition such as strep throat. Most sore throats are caused by viruses and are contagious.

Causes include:

- Viruses
- Strep bacteria
- Sleeping with mouth open

When You See

- Throat pain
- Swelling and redness of throat tissue
- Feeling tired
- Possible fever
- Possible difficulty swallowing or breathing

Do This First

1. Have child drink warm liquids and gargle frequently with warm salt water.
2. Use a cool-mist vaporizer to minimize pain.
3. Do not let child share toys or eating utensils.
4. See a healthcare provider for high or prolonged fever or for difficulty swallowing or breathing because of severe throat pain, or if the child breaks out in a skin rash.

Additional Care

- Follow your center's policy for giving children's acetaminophen or ibuprofen for pain (parental permission required)

Actions for parents:
- See a healthcare provider for fever, skin rash, or severe throat pain (antibiotics may be needed)
- Child with strep throat may return to school or childcare after 24 hours of antibiotic therapy if fever is gone

WHOOPING COUGH

Coughing is frequently a sign of a cold (see Colds section earlier) or other respiratory infection but may also occur with **whooping cough** (pertussis). Care for a child with whooping cough is described in this section.

Whooping cough is contagious. Young children are usually given a pertussis vaccine, but immunity may not last indefinitely.

Causes include:

- Bacterial infection

When You See

- In early stage: sneezing, nasal congestion, coughing
- Later stage (may last several weeks): uncontrollable bouts of coughing with whooping sound on inhalation

Do This First

1. Do not let child share toys or eating utensils.
2. A child suspected of having whooping cough should see a healthcare provider as soon as possible.

Additional Care

- Healthcare providers must report positive whooping cough cases
- Parents of other children in contact with sick child should be notified

Actions for parents:
- Take child to see a healthcare provider (antibiotic will be given)
- The healthcare provider will advise when child can return to school or childcare

EAR INFECTION

Middle-ear infections are the most common cause of ear pain in infants and young children, diminishing as the child grows older. Congestion in the eustachian tube, such as occurs with a cold, allows bacteria to grow. The infection puts pressure on the ear drum, causing pain. Ear infections are not contagious.

Causes include:

- Bacterial or viral infection

When You See

- Ear pain, pulling at or rubbing ear
- Irritability
- Possible fever
- Possible drainage from ear

Do This First

1. Follow your center's policy for giving children's acetaminophen or ibuprofen for pain (parental permission required).

2. Keep child upright to reduce pain.

Additional Care

- A covered hot water bottle or heating pad may help relieve pain

Actions for parents:

- Take child to see a healthcare provider (antibiotic will be given)
- Child can return to school or childcare when feeling well enough and fever has subsided

CHICKEN POX

Chicken pox is a common contagious disease that spreads easily among children. Chicken pox can cause considerable discomfort but seldom is a serious condition. A vaccine is available and is recommended for school-age children who have not had chicken pox. Having chicken pox confers immunity (**Figure 13-1**).

Causes include:

- Viral infection

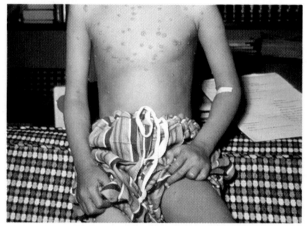

Figure 13-1 Chicken pox.

Learning
Checkpoint (1)

1. True or False: The best medicine for a child with a cold is aspirin.

2. See a healthcare provider for a child's sore throat if:

   a. The child has prolonged fever

   b. The child has a skin rash

   c. The child has difficulty swallowing

   d. All of the above

3. True or False: A child suspected of having whooping cough does not need to see a healthcare provider unless he or she experiences high fever.

4. How long should you wait before taking a child with an ear infection to a healthcare provider?

When You See

- A skin rash of itchy red spots, mostly on trunk and face
- Rash bumps break open, weep, then scab over
- Fever

Do This First

1. Keep child from scratching open the rash bumps.
2. Use calamine lotion or colloidal oatmeal for itching.
3. Keep child away from nonimmunized other children.

Additional Care

- Follow your center's policy for giving children's acetaminophen or ibuprofen for fever if needed (parental permission required)

Actions for parents:

- See a healthcare provider for high or persistent fever, rapid breathing, or other severe symptoms
- The child may return to school or childcare when all of the rash has dried and crusted

CONJUNCTIVITIS (PINKEYE)

Conjunctivitis, commonly called pinkeye, is an infection of the membranes inside the eyelids. This condition is contagious but usually not serious (**Figure 13-2**).

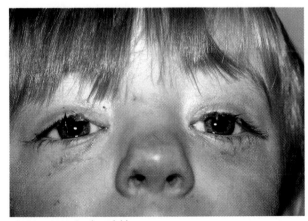

Figure 13-2 Conjunctivitis.

Causes include:

- Viral infection
- Bacterial infection
- Severe allergic condition

When You See

- One or both eyes look pink or red
- Yellow, green, or clear pus or drainage from eye(s)
- Eyelids may stick together after sleeping

Do This First

1. Keep child from rubbing eyes.
2. Child and others should wash hands frequently.
3. Do not let child share toys or eating utensils.
4. Carefully wash drainage from eyes with cotton ball or gauze soaked in warm water.

Additional Care

Actions for parents:

- See a healthcare provider since bacterial infection requires an antibiotic
- The child can return to school or childcare when drainage from the eyes stops, often after one to two days on an antibiotic

HEADACHE

Headaches are common in children. Headache may result from simple stress or fatigue, from various common illnesses such as a cold or the flu, or more rarely from a serious problem such as meningitis (see Chapter 8) or a head injury (see Chapter 6). Children may also have migraine headaches, which are recurring, severe, throbbing or stabbing headaches that may involve nausea and vomiting.

With a sudden, severe, unexplained headache, always look for a more serious cause. The following care is for nonemergency minor headaches.

Causes include:

- A cold or other infection
- Stress, fatigue
- Eye strain

When You See

- Child complains his or her head hurts
- Child may be holding head

Do This First

1. Have child rest quietly in darkened room.
2. Follow your center's policy for giving children's acetaminophen or ibuprofen (parental permission required).
3. Be alert for other symptoms.

Additional Care

Actions for parents:

- See a healthcare provider for recurring or severe headaches or for headache with stiff neck, marked irritability or lethargy, visual problems, a purple spotted rash, or repeated vomiting
- Child may attend school or childcare

DIARRHEA

Diarrhea in children is common and may result from a variety of different infections and conditions. Most often a viral infection of the stomach or intestines is the cause. Diarrhea can also result from other causes, including bacteria that are very contagious. Caregivers should wear gloves when changing diapers and wash hands frequently. When caused by infection, diarrhea may last several days to a week.

Causes include:

- Viral or bacterial infection
- Intestinal parasites
- Dietary changes
- Antibiotics

When You See

- Frequent loose, watery, or mushy stools
- Child may also vomit

Do This First

1. Keep the child well hydrated:
   a. Give an infant an electrolyte solution (such as Pedialyte™) between breast feedings; do not give infant formula for one or two feedings.
   b. Give a child an electrolyte solution (such as Pedialyte™) or a half-and-half mixture of a sports drink and water.
   c. If drinking fluids seems to increase vomiting, give fluid in small amounts frequently; have the child suck on ice chips.
2. With an infant, change the diaper immediately and wash the anal area well. A commercial product may minimize skin irritation.
3. Feed the child foods that minimize diarrhea, such as dry toast, bananas, crackers, applesauce (but not apple juice), rice, dry cereals, and other low-fat foods. Avoid milk, butter and margarine, cheese, and ice cream.

Additional Care

- Make sure the child uses good hygiene habits and washes hands well after using the bathroom

Actions for parents:

Call a healthcare provider and ask him or her when the child can return to school or childcare:

- If the diarrhea contains blood, pus, or mucus
- For an infant under six months old
- If the child seems dehydrated or very sick
- If the child cannot drink
- If the diarrhea lasts more than three days

CONSTIPATION

Constipation in children is usually temporary and not a sign of a serious condition. Constipation may occur, however, if another illness causes fever and vomiting that leads to dehydration.

Causes include:

- Changes in diet
- Not enough fiber in diet
- Dehydration or not drinking enough fluids

When You See

- Difficult bowel movements
- Hard, dry feces

Do This First

1. Have child drink plenty of fluids.
2. Ensure child's diet includes fruits and vegetables and other fiber-rich foods.

Additional Care

- For a toddler in toilet training, encourage child not to avoid bowel movements

Action for parents:

- See a healthcare provider if the child still has constipation after a week or has not had a bowel movement in four days

ALERT

Constipation

Do not give a child a laxative unless instructed by the healthcare provider.

STOMACHACHE

Stomachaches are common in young children, and some children may complain frequently. Usually the stomachache results from something minor, but occasionally the child may have a serious medical condition. Always monitor the child for other symptoms that may suggest a more serious condition (see Chapter 8). Also see the next section in this chapter on vomiting.

Learning
Checkpoint ②

1. True or False: Adult caregivers who had chicken pox as children need to be careful around children with chicken pox because their immunity may have worn off.

2. You can tell when a child's conjunctivitis is caused by bacteria because:

   a. The child will have a fever

   b. Drainage from the eye will be yellow

   c. The eye looks pink or red

   d. None of the above

3. True or False: Because of the risk of meningitis, all children with a headache should see a healthcare provider.

4. List at least three situations in which you should call a healthcare provider for a child who has diarrhea.

   _____

5. A child experiencing constipation should see a healthcare provider when he or she has not had a bowel movement in _____ days.

Causes include:

- Overeating
- Gas
- Stomach or intestinal infections
- Appendicitis and certain rare medical conditions

When You See

- Child complaining of stomach pain
- Child may be holding or rubbing stomach

Do This First

1. Have the child rest or lie down for 15 minutes.
2. Have the child hold a covered hot water bottle or heating pad on the stomach if this eases the pain.
3. Have a bowl or basin handy in case the child vomits.
4. Observe child for other symptoms.

Additional Care

- Do not give the child food (clear fluids are okay)

Actions for parents:

Call a healthcare provider if:

- The pain seems severe
- The pain lasts longer than two hours, or comes and goes for more than 12 hours
- Stomachaches are frequent
- The child vomits blood or a black or green substance
- There is blood in the stool
- The child has a high fever or signs of appendicitis

VOMITING

Vomiting, like nausea or stomachache, is usually a symptom of a viral infection. Diarrhea may also occur (see earlier sections on stomachache and diarrhea). As with diarrhea, the most important care is to prevent dehydration. The infection may be contagious.

Note that infants often "spit up" after being fed, particularly if not burped. This is not the same as vomiting, and the infant usually quickly recovers. An infant's repeated vomiting, however, can quickly lead to dehydration and become a medical emergency; in this case the infant should be taken to the hospital.

Causes include:

- Stomach or intestinal viral infection
- Dietary changes

When You See

- Child seems nauseous or says stomach hurts

Do This First

1. Be prepared for vomiting with a bowl or basin. Hold the child over the basin.
2. After the child vomits, wash around the mouth.
3. Do not give food or fluid for up to one hour, then let child slowly sip water or suck on ice chips.

Additional Care

- Let child rest or lie down, but do not feed right away. When the child is ready to eat, give bland foods (same as for diarrhea)
- Wear gloves when giving care, and wash hands afterwards. Have child also wash hands

Actions for parents:

Call a healthcare provider:

- For an infant under six months old
- If vomiting continues for six hours or more
- If the child has abdominal pain or fever
- If there is blood in the vomit
- If the child becomes dehydrated

URINARY TRACT INFECTION

Urinary tract infections occur when bacteria from the skin, gastrointestinal tract, or environment get into the urinary tract. These infections can be painful and uncomfortable but rarely become serious. Urinary tract infections are more common in girls than in boys. Occasionally pain-ful urination may occur with something other than a urinary tract infection, and a child needs to see a healthcare provider right away if there is also vomiting, back pain, fever, or shaking chills.

Causes include:

• Bacterial infection

When You See

• Pain, burning, or stinging on urination
• More frequent urination
• Possibly discolored urine

Do This First

1. Encourage the child to drink lots of fluids.
2. Ensure the child sees a healthcare provider.

Additional Care

Prevent urinary tract infections by:
• Teaching girls to wipe from front to back after going to the bathroom
• Not using bubble baths or strong soaps
• Having child wear only cotton underwear

Actions for parents:
• Take the child to a healthcare provider (antibi-otic treatment is needed)
• The child can attend school or childcare

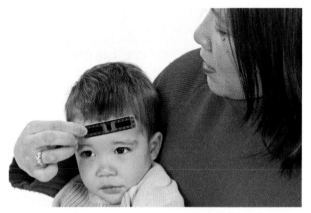

(a) Temperature strip

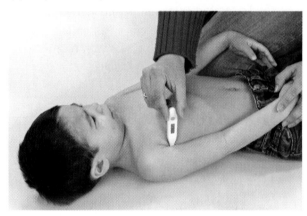

(b) Armpit (axillary) temperature

Figure 13-3 Checking for fever.

FEVER

Fever occurs often with viral or bacterial infec-tions ranging from colds to ear infections and sore throats. Fever is a sign the body is fighting the infection. A rapidly rising fever in a child can cause a seizure (see Chapter 8) or in an in-fant can cause dehydration.

Although temperature strips may be used on the forehead for infants or very small children, they are not as accurate as thermometers either in the mouth (over age four) or armpit (**Figure 13-3**). If possible, use a rectal thermometer for an infant (for

one minute). Allow three minutes for oral measure-ment or 10 for the armpit. Digital thermometers usually need only one minute for a reading.

The normal oral temperature is 98.6 degrees Fahrenheit. The normal underarm temperature is one degree lower, the normal rectal tempera-ture one degree higher.

Causes include:

• Viral or bacterial infection
• Heat exhaustion or heatstroke (see Chapter 10)
• Some medications or poisons (see Chapter 9)
• Extreme exertion

When You See

- A child's temperature more than one or two degrees above normal

Do This First

1. Since the child may have a contagious disease, have him or her rest away from other children.
2. Give the child lots of clear fluids.
3. For a fever over 101 degrees Fahrenheit, follow your center's policy for giving children's acetaminophen or ibuprofen if needed for the child's comfort (parental permission required).
4. For a fever over 103 degrees Fahrenheit, cool the child by sponging the skin with room-temperature water; avoid chilling.

Additional Care

- Observe the child for other symptoms and treat accordingly

Actions for parents:

See a healthcare provider if:

- An infant under three months old has a fever above 100 degrees Fahrenheit
- The fever lasts more than 24 hours in a child under 12 months old
- An older child's fever is 104 degrees Fahrenheit or higher
- Any fever lasts more than five days
- The child has other serious symptoms such as a stiff neck, confusion, extreme irritability or lethargy, severe sore throat or headache, ear pain, repeated diarrhea or vomiting, or rapid breathing
- The child can return to school or childcare 24 hours after the fever ends, or when approved by the healthcare provider

ALERT

Fever

Do not give a child aspirin because of the danger of Reye syndrome. Follow your center's policy for giving children's acetaminophen or ibuprofen if needed (parental permission required).

Diaper Rash

Diaper rash is a common, often painful skin irritation caused by exposure to wet diapers (Figure 13-4). It can be prevented by frequently changing a child's diaper and using good hygiene practices. The rash usually clears up in two to three days. Occasionally a more severe infection may occur, extending outside the diaper area or causing blisters.

Causes include:

- Wet diapers

When You See

- A red rash in the diaper area
- Pain in the area

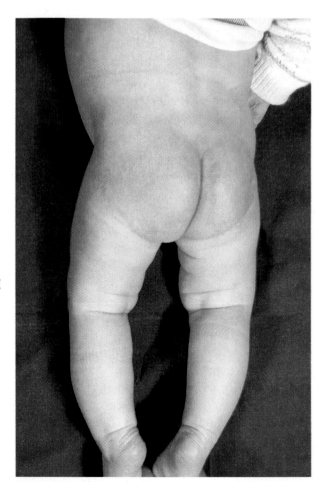

Figure 13-4 Diaper rash.

Do This First

1. Keep the skin dry by changing diapers often; do not use plastic pants. Leave diapers off as long as possible between changing.
2. Wash the area with mild soap and water. Soaking in water may help. Dry thoroughly before putting on a fresh diaper.
3. Rash may be prevented with zinc oxide, ointment, or petroleum jelly, but do not put ointment on an existing rash (may delay healing). Do not use baby powder or talc because of the risk of the infant inhaling it.

Additional Care

- Wear gloves when changing diapers, and wash hands afterward

- Rinse cloth diapers with vinegar solution to remove irritating ammonia

Actions for parents:
- Call a healthcare provider if blisters are present, the rash is outside the diaper area, or the rash continues longer than three days
- The child can attend school or childcare

COLD SORE

Cold sores are oozing blisters that can form anywhere on the body but are most common on the lips or inside the mouth. The infection is transmitted by contact, including through saliva, and cannot be cured. After the initial infection the virus stays inside the person, and cold sores

Learning Checkpoint 3

1. Check off situations in which a healthcare provider should be called for a child experiencing stomachache: (Check all that apply.)

___ The pain is severe   ___ The child ate too much ice cream

___ The child vomits blood   ___ The pain has lasted 30 minutes

___ The child has a high fever   ___ The child is sleepy

2. How long should a child who has just vomited wait before drinking fluids?

_____

3. Name two common signs of a urinary tract infection.

_____

4. Cool down a child with a fever over 103 degrees Fahrenheit by:

   a. Putting the child in a bathtub of cold water

   b. Putting ice packs in the child's armpits and groin area

   c. Sponging the child's skin with room-temperature water

   d. Any of the above

5. True or False: Apply zinc oxide to a diaper rash to promote healing.

reappear occasionally. An outbreak may be triggered by many factors, including cold or heat, stress, or fever. The sores form scabs and heal in one to two weeks (**Figure 13-5**).

Causes include:

- The herpes simplex virus

When You See

- Watery blisters on or near lips or in mouth
- Pain or itching

Do This First

1. Keep child from picking at or scratching the sores.

2. Child and caregivers should wash hands frequently.

3. Relieve discomfort with lip balm.

Additional Care

Actions for parents:

- A young child who is likely to touch the sores and spread the virus to others should be kept home until the sores are scabbed over, unless they can be covered.
- An older child who understands the importance of not touching the sores can attend school or childcare.

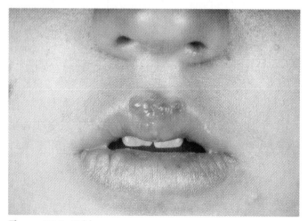

Figure 13-5 Cold sore.

TOOTHACHE

Toothache usually results from teething or cavities. A very young child may have tooth decay caused by having a bottle of milk or something sweet before naps or bedtime; this is sometimes called "bottlemouth." A child may sometimes not be able to identify the source of pain, however, and may have an earache, sore throat, or other condition. Watch for other symptoms that may suggest a medical rather than dental problem.

Causes include:

- Tooth decay, cavities
- New teeth coming through

When You See

- Tooth pain
- Possible low fever

Do This First

1. Inspect the mouth for any obvious problems. A swollen jaw and redness around the tooth may indicate an abscess that needs to be seen by a healthcare provider.

2. Follow your center's policy for giving children's acetaminophen or ibuprofen for pain (parental permission required). For teething pain, other commercial products may help.

3. Have child lie down with jaw against a covered hot water bottle or heating pad.

Additional Care

Actions for parents:

- Make a dental appointment for the child
- See a healthcare provider if the child also has an earache or fever of 102 degrees Fahrenheit or higher
- Without fever, the child can attend school or childcare

SKIN RASHES

Skin rashes and problems that cause rashes occur often in children. More than a dozen different common ailments can produce skin conditions loosely called a rash, making it often difficult to know for sure what is causing the child's skin problem. Fortunately, most skin problems are minor.

You cannot always, and sometimes not even usually, diagnose a rash based solely on its appearance, because there are so many different causes and the appearance may vary from child to child. The diagnosis often depends on other information, including:

- How the rash began
- Where it appears on the body
- How it spread
- Associated symptoms such as itching or fever
- Factors to which the child has been exposed

Treatment guidelines are based on the severity of the child's symptoms and the cause of the rash. Minor rashes that cause only minor discomfort may not require any treatment beyond observation. More serious rashes may be contagious or cause symptoms troubling enough to require treatment.

The following information is intended only as general information. Unless you are sure of the cause of a child's rash based on your experience, leave the diagnosis and treatment decisions to a healthcare provider.

Causes include:

- *Prickly heat* (heat rash). More common in very young children, little red bumps appear at sweat glands; treated by keeping child in cooler, less humid environment.
- *Diaper rash.* See earlier section in this chapter.
- *Hives.* An allergic reaction caused by certain foods, medications, even stress; can be emergency if breathing difficulty occurs (see Allergic Reactions in Chapter 4).
- *Poison ivy.* See Chapter 9.
- *Eczema.* A condition of dry, itching skin, often with family history, that may make young children scratch and cause infections.

- *Acne.* Common at puberty, usually unrelated to diet (a common myth).
- *Athlete's foot.* A fungal infection, commonly transmitted in locker-rooms or shower facilities.
- *Cradle cap.* A form of seborrhea, or dandruff. Mild redness and scaling or crusting patches on scalp or behind ears of young infants.
- *Chicken pox.* See earlier section in this chapter.
- *Measles.* Highly contagious viral disease causing a spreading red rash; rare now because of standard immunization.
- *Rubella* (German measles). Red rash caused by a mild viral infection, less contagious than measles, usually does not require treatment.
- *Roseola.* Caused by a viral infection that produces high fever and sometimes other symptoms before the rash appears; usually a mild disease, but is contagious.

In addition, rashes can be caused by the following five conditions.

Fifth Disease

Fifth disease is a contagious viral infection that usually causes no symptoms other than the rash (**Figure 13-6**). For most children it is a mild disease without complications and with no need for treatment. It can present a risk, however, to pregnant women or children with certain chronic illness.

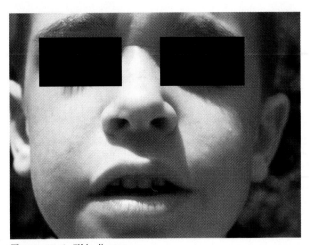

Figure 13-6 Fifth disease.

When You See

- Bright red rash usually beginning on cheeks ("slapped cheek" appearance), later spreading to arms and legs

Do This First

1. Watch the child for other symptoms.
2. Try to prevent the infection spreading through direct contact.

Additional Care

Actions for parents:

- Monitor child and take his or her temperature often; see a healthcare provider if fever or other symptoms occur
- The child need not stay home

Impetigo

Impetigo is a skin infection by streptococcal or other bacteria (**Figure 13-7**). The child feels very itchy and may scratch the area, then transmitting the infection to other body areas. It is easily transmitted to other children as well. Usually the infection is harmless, but a rare complication can cause a kidney problem (glomerulonephritis).

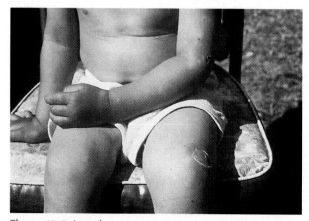

Figure 13-7 Impetigo.

When You See

- Small red spots that progress to blisters that ooze and produce yellow-brown crusts
- Itchiness

Do This First

1. Prevent the child from scratching; child should wash hands often.
2. Wash and soak the area with soap and warm water to remove the crusts.
3. Follow your center's policy to apply a topical antibiotic ointment.
4. Prevent direct contact with others.

Additional Care

- Monitor the child for any other symptoms and healing of the rash within a few days

Actions for parents:

- Call a healthcare provider if the rash does not improve in a few days, if the child has any other symptoms, or if the child's urine turns dark brown
- The child can return to school or childcare a day after beginning to use the antibiotic ointment

Ringworm

Ringworm is a contagious fungal infection (that has nothing to do with worms). It spreads by direct contact. Ringworm can usually be treated with appropriate over-the-counter products (**Figure 13-8**).

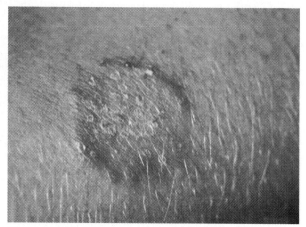

Figure 13-8 Ringworm.

When You See

- Rash begins as small round red spots that grow and become ring-shaped, with the ring border red, raised, and scaly
- If the scalp is involved (rare), hair may fall out temporarily

Do This First

1. Keep child from touching the area; avoid direct contact with others.
2. Wearing gloves, apply an antifungal ointment intended for ringworm (follow your center's policies).
3. Have child wash hands frequently.

Additional Care

Actions for parents:

- See a healthcare provider if the ringworm shows no improvement or keeps spreading after a week of treatment
- While being treated, the child can attend school or childcare

Scabies

Scabies is a skin condition caused by tiny mites, related to chiggers, that dig into the skin and cause red bumps and severe itching (**Figure 13-9**). Typically the knee and elbow creases, armpits, and webbing between toes and fingers are affected. The infestation spreads by direct contact or indirect contact with a person's infested clothing. The child is likely to scratch the areas, which may then become infected.

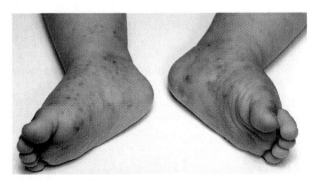

Figure 13-9 Scabies.

When You See

- Severe itching
- Red bumps that may become oozing sores or blisters

Do This First

1. Give cool baths and use compresses or calamine to sooth itching.
2. The child needs to see a healthcare provider for a prescription anti-mite medication.

Additional Care

Actions for parents:

- All the child's bedding and clothing, including coats and hats, should be washed in hot water and dried on high heat. Use a hot dryer for stuffed toys, pillows, and cushions.
- Vacuum and clean all items and areas with which the child had contact in a childcare center, in the home, and in the family car. Anything that cannot be cleaned or heated in a clothes dryer should be sealed for two weeks in plastic bags.
- Follow the healthcare provider's instructions for treatment with prescription ointment
- One day after beginning the treatment the child can return to school or childcare

Scarlet Fever

Scarlet fever is caused by a streptococcal infection. Fever and fatigue often occur before the rash, along with headache, nausea, and vomiting. About 12 to 48 hours later the rash begins on the face, trunk, and arms and spreads to cover much of the body. The infection is contagious and spreads by direct contact or indirect contact when the victim sneezes (**Figure 13-10**).

When You See

- Intense red rash of tiny bumps lasting five days or more; skin then peels
- Tongue first has a white coating, and then turns red and swollen

- Red throat, and red spots on roof of mouth
- Sore throat

Do This First

1. Have child drink lots of fluids.
2. Follow your center's policy for giving children's acetaminophen or ibuprofen for high fever (parental permission required).
3. Prevent contact with other children, and encourage child to wash hands often.

Additional Care

Actions for parents:

- Take the child to a healthcare provider (an antibiotic will be prescribed)
- The child may return to school or childcare one day after starting the antibiotic, if fever has passed

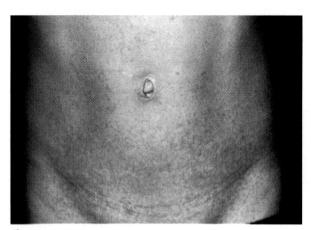

Figure 13-10 Scarlet fever.

HEAD LICE

Head lice can occur on any child and are highly contagious. They spread by direct contact or through sharing hats, hairbrushes, or even coats touching when hung together (**Figure 13-11**).

When You See

- Frequent scratching of head
- Child complains of scalp itching
- Pinpoint red marks on scalp
- Tiny clusters of eggs (nits) like white lumps on hair

Do This First

1. Parents should use over-the-counter head lice shampoo, carefully following the product's directions; some products require multiple applications.
2. Family members, playmates, and others in contact with the child must be carefully checked for nits or signs of lice; all should be treated at the same time.

Additional Care

Actions for parents:

- All the child's bedding and clothing, including coats and hats, should be washed in hot water and dried on high heat. Use a hot dryer for stuffed toys, pillows, and cushions.
- Vacuum and clean all items and areas with which the child had contact in a childcare center, in the home, and in the family car. Anything that cannot be cleaned or heated in a clothes dryer should be sealed for two weeks in plastic bags.
- The child can return to school or childcare after complete treatment for head lice, following the site's specific policy.

Figure 13-11 Head lice.

Head Lice

Do not use lice shampoo on an infant.
Wear gloves when using lice shampoo.

Learning
Checkpoint (4)

1. True or False: A toddler with an oozing cold sore on his lip should be kept at home until the sore scabs over.

2. If a child has a toothache, what two other symptoms require seeing a healthcare provider rather than making a dental appointment?

_____

3. True or False: Since most skin rashes are signs of serious illness, always see a healthcare provider immediately for a child with any kind of rash.

4. True or False: Because fifth disease is contagious, a child in a childcare center with a red rash with a "slapped face" appearance should be taken home immediately.

5. True or False: A topical antibiotic is used for impetigo.

6. Describe what to do with a child who has ringworm.

_____

7. A child with scabies can have the condition again, even after correctly using prescribed anti-mite medication, if the parents fail to do what?

_____

8. What symptoms usually precede the rash of scarlet fever? Check all that apply.

___ Fever   ___ Confusion, disorientation

___ Brown-colored urine   ___ Headache

___ Nausea, vomiting   ___ Constipation

9. True or False: Because there are no symptoms, a child can have head lice for months before anyone realizes it.

Index